THE HANGOVER

Overcoming Emotional Addiction

12- Steps for Emotional Sobriety

Dr. Carleah East, LMHC

THE HANGOVER
Overcoming Emotional Addiction - 12- Steps for Emotional Sobriety

ISBN-13: 978-0692988923
ISBN-10: 0692988920

Publishing and Editing by: SheEO Publishing Co.

Cover and Interior Design: SheEO Publishing Company
www.SheEOPublishing.com

Author Photo: Shutter Nduljence Photography © All Rights Reserved

Dr. Carleah East's, titles may be purchased in bulk for educational, business, fund-raising, or sales promotional use. For information or other products and services, contact Dr. Carleah East at www.TheSapphireWoman.com

Printed in the United States of America

DEDICATION

To every woman who has ever been loved or given love. Know that your worth is not determined by another's estimate, but is validated by your presence each and every day. Continue to inspire the world with your perfectly imperfect ways, unique styles and feisty wit. Remember: there's only one like you! So SMILE, fix your CROWN and SLAY IN YOUR LANE!

ACKNOWLEDGEMENTS

To my supportive husband, son, mother, and father. Each one of you has encouraged me to speak my truth without hesitation. I thank you for allowing my tears to sometimes fall without judgment and for your unconditional love.

To my crew: Best friends, sisters, riders, and shenanigan explorers. Each one of you bring out the best in me and the laughter is endless.

To my professional team: Indeed, it takes a village and I am so grateful to each of you for believing in my vision and promoting my passion.

To my doubters: Thanks for thinking of me.

Praise for Dr. East

I made an appointment with Dr. East because I knew I needed some help when it comes to relationships. I had just gotten out of a toxic relationship. The only problem was, I didn't see it as toxic. I blamed myself for everything that went wrong in that relationship, I was broken, I was emotional, and I had given up. I didn't know my self-worth and definitely needed help finding that. Dr. East helped me realize that just because you are in one toxic relationship, it does not mean you will continue that pattern. She helped me to see that you can break free of that cycle and that loving yourself is the first place to start. Dr. East helped me to see myself for ME, not for who I am when I am in a relationship. She showed me I am more than just a girlfriend; I am more than just a pawn in an abusive relationship. I cannot thank her enough for all she has done to help me be the best me I can be.

-Amy Sapanara-

Dr. East is that objective voice that, over the past few months, has equipped me with the tools to face, tackle, and unravel the inner-self. Together, we have worked through these stirrings one by one, not skipping steps, and setting realistic, attainable goals. By working with Dr. East, I have come to learn vulnerability is one of my greatest strengths, and that to be self-aware and open takes courage. Dr. East helped me to understand the stereotypes that women struggle with. We are expected to be strong but submissive, independent but not assertive or aggressive, successful but not too successful, and delicate but not fragile. One of the most difficult misconceptions I've had to confront and change is that we as women are taught that we are responsible for the actions and egos of others. We are not. All in all, at the root of all the little lessons that Dr. East has taught me is that "it's ok to not be ok from time to time."

-Jarik Melendez-

TABLE OF CONTENTS

*"Don't Let Others Define You,
For You Are Your Own Definition."*

~Dr. East

PROLOGUE

*I*magine this:

Coming in from a night of drunken indulgence, you wake up in the morning with a pounding headache and feel like crap. You believe that if you have another drink, it will alleviate the pain. This avoidance of substance pain is the same avoidance used when dealing with emotional pain. But instead of having another drink, you have another encounter. All to avoid The Hangover.

When it comes to emotional addiction, it can be difficult to recognize the signs and symptoms.

This 12-step guide walks you through the ups and downs of emotional addiction. Not only will you be able to identify the signs, but also the steps necessary for recovery.

Recovery is not simply about the removal of a drug.

Recovery is about the many sensory influences that are involved in withdrawal.

If you are an emotional addict or know one, you should be aware of some, if not all, of the emotional aspects that can pull one's senses in multiple directions.

Think about this for a second: Love is a high. And because that love can sometimes cause pain, pain can also become a high.

Emotional addiction occurs when your body gets used to the emotional ups and downs associated with certain situations or relationships. Eventually, your emotional chemistry changes and that type of "emotional roller coaster" becomes normal to you.

The only way to overcome the emotional roller coaster of addiction is to go to rehab. But the withdrawal phase can make doing this quite difficult.

Normally, in a toxic or addictive relationship, a person will habitually revert back for "fixes." You get your concentrated fix (or your "high") by engaging in simple behaviors, which allow you to still have contact with your drug of choice (i.e. the person you are in love with).

Although you may have chosen to separate yourself from that person, you break the rules and continue to communicate with each other sporadically. The communication can be via texting, video chatting, sending cards and flowers, calling on a special occasion, or even meeting for drinks every now and then. These methods of communication or encounters, which you may consider innocent, are your "fixes" (or hits) which you take, so you don't have to experience the emotional trauma of withdrawal or The Hangover.

STEP 1

AM I AN **EMOTIONAL ADDICT?**

*A*n emotional addict is an individual who is addicted and emotionally attracted to the highs and lows of a relationship. When this happens, the emotional chemistry in the affected individual's brain and receptors create an addiction. As a result, the addict adjusts him or herself to a "roller coaster" of emotions and feelings.

An emotional "roller coaster high" occurs when you are happy and feel like your relationship is at its peak (the good times). Likewise, an emotional "roller coaster low" happens when you are sad and feel like your relationship is at its lowest point (the bad times). Without even realizing it, you become emotionally immune and dependent on the cycle of emotional ups and downs.

Another example of you being on an emotional roller coaster ride is when you try to break up with someone. It's likely that you've experienced a downward spiral of emotions. To make yourself feel better again, you may feel like you need to go back to the individual to get an emotional re-up. A re-up can be described as you getting a "fix" from another person. This cycle is similar to when a person struggles with substance addiction and experiences a relapse. It is during the "fixation" period that you will experience a few days of perfect bliss and happiness. This is called the "honeymoon" period in the relationship. This is where you will be deceived and made to believe that you're receiving the love, affection, happiness, and safety of your partner. Without warning, the "honeymoon" period abruptly comes to an end because the repeated, vicious cycle of emotional abuse has reared its ugly head.

Unfortunately, many women are unable to move on from this type of emotional addiction, as it tends to be the residual base of every relationship that you get involved in. You will find yourself in a perfectly positive relationship while still finding things that are wrong. Why? There may be several reasons as to why you are struggling with this type of emotional behavior. However, the main one could be that you still haven't dealt with the emotional trauma of your previous relationships.

It could also be that you are distracting yourself by jumping from relationship to relationship because you are trying to avoid the root cause of the situation: the first onset of trauma that you encountered. Another possibility is that you've decided to stay with the same person because by staying, there is necessarily little or no effort involved. You have allowed yourself to believe that there are not any lost feelings and that there is a level of comfort within the relationship.

Unbeknownst to you, this type of emotional behavior becomes a systematic cycle of repetitive negative relationships. It just goes on and on and ultimately bleeds over into your current and future relationships. Once it seeps into your relationships, it will eventually cause those relationships to spiral downward, and fast!

How to Determine if You're an Emotional Addict

Allow yourself to see patterns in your relationships. Write both the good and bad things that happen in your relationship in your journal on a regular basis. Often a person can't see the forest for the trees because of how immersed they are in something. However, when you have a point of reference it allows you to pinpoint the trouble areas in your relationship.

Dissect what exactly occurred during the good and bad cycles. There may be patterns that emerge. For instance, if you are constantly trying to get your partner involved in some things that you want to do and without any consideration, he or she refuses to do it, that pattern should be viewed as a bad cycle. If they are open to your suggestions and ideas, then that should be viewed as a good cycle. What if your partner is frequently unwilling to compromise with you on something because they have prior plans and you feel left out? Think about it. How often do they do things without you? How often do you get upset about it? Is your relationship a partnership or a dictatorship? You must really discern these and other patterns of behavior in the relationship. Sit down and honestly ask yourself, "Are there patterns of ups and downs in this relationship?" Do not sweep them under the rug as if they do not exist. They are relevant.

Get assessments from people that you care about. Sometimes you do have to consider the advice of your close family members and friends to point the things out that you don't see with your own eyes. Your trusted advisors will be honest with you and will let you know when you're not on task with certain parts of your relationship. Ask them to evaluate you on your behaviors, responses, and whether you're being extra or passive aggressive. By seeking their advice, this will better assist you in determining if you are dealing with the characteristics of emotional addiction.

Below are several ways you can recognize your addictive behaviors:

Do you keep dating the same prototype (a different person who has the same characteristics as your former mate)? Do you find yourself continuously changing partners? Do you have a specific prototype or definition that you set for yourself? Oftentimes, such actions indicate you're afraid or simply do not know how to step outside of your emotional box. You tend to gravitate towards familiar things and people with whom you are comfortable and share similar characteristics. Think about the characteristics that your past relationships have in common.

Overcome denial and admit your addiction is critical. Denial is a large part of any type of addiction. Sometimes your self-deception or perception does not allow you to admit that you have a problem. You may think there's nothing wrong with your life or relationship while so many things in your life seem to be spiraling out of control. It may be difficult, but admitting you have a problem is necessary.

Realize that admitting your addiction or problem is not a sign of weakness. Oftentimes, an individual does not admit there's a problem because it may be seen as a weakness. Additionally, society often plays an attack game against women where women are deemed responsible for the relationship's success, or are responsible for making the house a home. There are all these pressures on women and, oftentimes, we don't want to admit there's a problem. We don't want to feel weak like we can't handle our relationships or ourselves. Thus, getting out of that mindset and recognizing that admitting your addiction is a process of strength rather than a weakness ultimately adds to your growth and maturity as a woman. Getting this thought process inside of your head is a key step.

Think and ask yourself these honest and straight-up questions. "Okay, there's nothing wrong with me, but things are just popping off. Things are not going well. Things are spiraling, so what is the root cause of the spiral?" "What is the primary issue concerning all of these areas of my life? Am I having difficulties in my relationship with my partner, my family and the people at work?" Honestly ask yourself: are you the common denominator and root cause in many of the situations you are facing?

The patterns you see throughout these areas can help you to overcome denial. In the same respect, sometimes you have to hit certain markers in your life in order to admit that you need help. Admitting you have a problem is actually one of the first steps to overcoming your problem. You must be open to learning how to adopt new tools to resolve your issue. Also, you must change your thought process on how you see problems. Problems have such a negative connotation to them. You hear the word "problem" or hear the word "consequence" and immediately think, "Oh, I don't want any of that". But, in life, women are transitioning all the time. Every day there's a transition. Every day there is someone who comes into your life who negatively or positively impacts you. With a different mindset and way of behaving, you can grow and become an emotionally stable individual. So instead of just viewing your life's situations as problems, learn to view them as challenges. When you say, "I'm being challenged", there's a positive connotation to that statement. In effect, you are saying, "Okay, if I'm being challenged, then I can overcome the challenge". And if you tell yourself, "I don't have a problem, but instead I have a challenge", then you are reframing how you see those situations. Changing your mindset is vital because it will change your perspective on how you deal with and overcome your issues and addictions.

Types of Addictive Behaviors That Can Affect Your Physical and Mental Health

Addictive behaviors focus on your life and the things that you are emotionally addicted to. Whether it be mentally, physically, socially, or professionally, emotional addictions can hold you hostage in any area of your life.

Addictive behaviors can lead an individual into an emotionally abusive relationship. Within that type of relationship, one may find themselves on both sides of the spectrum, both as the victim and the perpetrator.

Suppressive. The act of being suppressive occurs when you push things out of your conscience and into your subconscious because you don't want to deal with them.

Unfortunately, the problem with this is that you may suppress areas that could bring you awareness. Often, you end up compartmentalizing. Imagine the emotional part of your brain as an apartment complex. It has thirty-two units in it, and each one is a place where you store an experience, emotion, or feeling that you don't want to deal with. You don't want to deal with them because you've got to go to work, get the kids ready, or because they are painful. Either way, you don't want to process the pain. So now, all thirty-two apartments are filled, but you're still dealing with these emotional experiences. Where do those new emotions go?

When you suppress and compartmentalize negative experiences, emotions, or feelings, you end up filling your cup until it overflows, lashing out at others, having a mental breakdown, or suffering an emotional relapse. When you compartmentalize things instead of dealing with them head-on, you are telling yourself, "No, I'm not going to deal with these issues". This emotional avoidance is a characteristic of addictive behavior, which hinders your emotional well-being and causes emotional overload.

Rationalization. When you rationalize, you are making excuses for behaviors that are taking place. You either rationalize your own behavior or the behavior of your partner. By rationalizing, you give your mate a pass. For example, if your mate communicates with you in a disrespectful tone, you might rationalize it by saying, "Well they probably had a bad day, so I'm going to ignore the fact that they were disrespectful." Perhaps you tell yourself, "Maybe my tone could have been nicer; Maybe I could have cleaned a little bit better;" or "Maybe if I had cared a little bit more, they wouldn't have responded that way." By rationalizing their behavior, you end up rationalizing your own.

Have you ever disrespected someone and then made excuses for your behavior? Did you rationalize it by saying, "Well, because they did this, this, and this, I responded the way I did?" Maybe you said, "This is the way I've always been, which is why I responded that way."

Rationalization gives you excuses to continue to behave in negative ways, or continue to accept negative behavior from others.

Competition. When you have mistrust, envy, and jealousy towards other women, it will affect you emotionally. It will cause you to automatically lay a foundation of mistrust in your relationships. Those feelings will then impact how you interact with other women and how you present yourself in front of each other. Because of this, you will allow yourself to remain in unhealthy relationships for a number of reasons. One reason could be to prove a point to another woman or show others that you have your life together. The problem with that is no one will admit that they are struggling with challenges in their relationship. Ultimately, neither you nor the other woman who is struggling will open up enough to talk about what you both are experiencing. If you did open up, you would likely realize that there are other people going through the same things that you are--just on a different level.

Competitiveness also stops us from being authentic. Essentially, you're getting up every day and putting on a costume-- a presentation, so to speak. Because of that presentation, you will not allow yourself to be honest about who you are, what you are experiencing, and that you are a fallible creature. Do you walk around in a "zipped up" costume with hair, clothes, jewelry and a smile? Once you get home, do you peel all that stuff off to find that you're an empty or cracked shell? As you now may have realized, a lot of that needing to compete with other women stops you from being authentic, and you end up "faking it until you make it". That daily perspective eventually becomes a way that you mentally address everything. What's really going on is, there's this internal phase of pain that you're totally concealing and never deal with because you choose to present a cover-up. Eventually you experience a buildup. Just like a volcano, you erupt. You erupt on your family and co-workers. You lose it and snap for no apparent reason. You randomly cry at times when there's nothing said because you're suffering from an emotional overload and are not being authentic or true to yourself.

Fear of Being Alone. Society sends negative messages to women about there being a limited amount of potential mates. That message alone causes women to compete to gain a mate. Likewise, society tells you that you need to present yourself in the best light possible to even be considered worthy of another person's affection or to win a mate. Women are not always taught that they are the prize or a person of value. Some women have been taught and are constantly warned: "You don't want to be an old cat lady dying alone." For some women, they have a fear of being alone. Some will even admit that they're incomplete without a mate. Unfortunately, that's the reason why some women find themselves serial dating and going from person to person in relationships.

Some women even meet and go on dates with people they don't find interesting or attractive. They do this for the sake of saying, "I'm going on a date" to avoid being lonely. However, when you're alone in your own space, you have time to reflect, think, and look at yourself in the mirror. When you can do that, you are able to see who you really are. You may painfully realize that you're living a lie, and that you must allow yourself to remove the mask. Any situation that causes you to look yourself in the mirror can help you avoid self-sabotage.

Distraction. Working can become a distraction, which, in turn, becomes another addictive behavior. A woman may distract herself by constantly working or going to the gym. Women tend to dedicate lots of time to their outer core while neglecting the equally important work on their inner core.

You may not realize it, but when you suppress, compete, and rationalize negative behavior or situations, the cycle of addictive behavior takes control of your life. Furthermore, having the fear of being alone will often lead to your finding ways to distract yourself in order to avoid facing the real issues. These are all triggers, which will cause the cycle of addictive behavior to continue in your life.

Abuse. Emotional abuse is often unrecognizable because you can't visualize the pain that has been inflicted. Regardless of whether you've experienced physical abuse, in most cases you can identify it. Despite this, you may ignore abusive relationships that don't leave a physical mark. You often won't recognize the fact that you're in an abusive relationship. Physical abuse is not always the gateway. The gateway is that initial crack in your surface of emotional instability.

Emotional abuse occurs when your mate repeatedly says derogatory statements to you that are hurtful. They may call you stupid, or try to discredit your opinion by saying that you're being dramatic, or that you're over reacting. They may constantly criticize your appearance or accomplishments. They may frequently compare you to others as a way of discrediting your feelings. Taking this into consideration, you may say, "Well, maybe I am overreacting or being dramatic." What you don't realize is that emotional abuse is a tactic that others use to stop you from being expressive.

The next thing you know, emotional abuse is followed by physical abuse. Let's say it happens once and your thought process is, "I'm going to give them a chance. Everybody makes mistakes". Responses like that are embedded in your DNA: "Everybody makes mistakes, let's forgive and work on the relationship." Additionally, your abuser will groom you by saying, "I'm sorry that I did that." They may even continue to be nice for a while.

However, they will eventually abuse you again. You grow accustomed to the abuse little by little, and it ends up destroying your self-esteem, self-concept, and self-worth.

The abuse devalues you and makes you more susceptible to believing what your partner is telling you. Then, the next time they tell you, "You're stupid," you will actually reason with yourself by saying, "You know what, that probably was a stupid comment. Let me work on that." At that very moment, your abuser has become the dictator of how you view yourself as a person.

You become accepting of that type of behavior, that type of talk, and that type of treatment. When your mate imposes physical abuse upon you, never tell yourself, "Well, this is just one time. We have invested time in this relationship, and we do have good times."

Some women get so accustomed to being physically and emotionally abused, they can't handle a relationship where there's not a physical altercation. They grow too used to being on the emotional roller coaster.

Your past, especially your upbringing at home, is another huge gateway for accepting physical and emotional abuse. Some women who were raised in dysfunctional or abusive homes may find themselves going from relationship to relationship because they didn't have a positive parental environment. Because these women didn't necessarily get those lessons of self-worth and value through their parents, they now tend to cling onto relationships to get that "father figure" or "strong female figure" from their partners. The women find themselves in relationships where their partner dominates. This represents the inner-child in them that never got that firm emotional connection of love from their parents. Their choice of mate/abuser will be controlling, aggressive, and dogmatic. Initially these characteristics provide women with a false sense of security.

Contrarily, it may very well be that the abuser was abused in their childhood. They never received therapy for it or never talked about it. Sadly, they may have never even realized it was abuse. Maybe their mother was just extra abusive or heavy-handed. Maybe they were sexually abused by their parent and were never taught that type of behavior was inappropriate. Maybe they had a mom or a dad that made an excuse for the abuse in their own relationship and came to believe that, "A healthy relationship may involve someone hitting you from time to time, but that doesn't mean that you leave." These negative examples that they've seen become the baseline of how they manage their own relationships. Due to that harsh upbringing, the abused tends to seek control in relationships, and can become abusive.

This gateway of emotional abuse can also bleed into other areas such as sexual and spiritual abuse. Thus, the cycle of abuse continues; at times you are the victim, and at times you are the perpetrator.

Reflections
Step 1
Am I An Emotional Addict?

STEP 2

SOCIETY IS YOUR
PUSHER MAN

- $\mathcal{S}$ociety and how it has created a dynamic desperation in women;

- Continuous references to women's inadequacy and inability to fit the "status quo mold" of looks, income, etc.;

- How women are constantly bombarded with messages that enforce the notion that it's hard to find a good mate;

- Historical concepts and expectations of women in general and how these expectations and limitations have shaped women's overall thought processes and approaches to relationships and love.

The Definition of a Pusher Man

What is a Pusher Man?   A Pusher Man is a street pharmacist also known as a "drug dealer."   In this chapter, we will learn how society has become the Pusher Man to many women.   You will also discover how the constant subliminal messages (the harmful "drugs") that society pushes to women can endanger, negatively influence, and hinder their lives.

Types of Societal Drugs and Their Harmful Effects

1. **Acting or Looking a Certain Way.** The first pill or drug that society gives you influences you to believe that you need to look, act, and behave a particular way. Society's messages influence women by telling them that they need to lose weight and that they shouldn't accept their own bodies. They influence women about how they are supposed to present themselves to the world.

   When you look at advertising, it focuses on women most of the time. Most magazine articles are all about the right lipstick, the right shade of eye shadow, the right tan lines, and being a certain weight. Society has made up a fictitious character that women often try to live up to. Women, in turn, suffer from low self-esteem because they compare themselves to the women they see on television or in magazines. Additionally, magazine articles influence women on how they can look younger and how they can be more appealing and attractive. Society's constant barrage of messages influence you on how you need to fix your outer appearance to attract mates. Think about it: how often have you read magazines that encourage emotional healing? Have you ever experienced low self-esteem because you didn't have the body shape or certain look that society convinced you that you needed to have? My point exactly.

2. **The Perfect Mate Fantasy.** The second pill that society pushes on women influences you to believe what a

mate looks like and what a mate should be. Because of this, you will often find yourself with someone that everybody else thinks is great for you, but with whom you know you're not truly happy with. And when I say happy, I'm not talking about the monetary or "buy me trinkets" happy, but the Netflix with no-chill happy. Damn the sex and the tangible items, you're just happy spending time with your boo. Now that's happy!

All the negative connotations that society and others push on you is to make you feel like you don't measure up and can't fit in. Based on other people's misconceptions and pre-conceived ideas, you will:

1. Create a fictional character of someone that is perfect for you as a mate. But, in reality, that individual is 10% of your family's expectations, 15% of society's views, 5% of what you really want and the other 70%...well, the rest of that shit is from Barbie and her dream life created by Mattel!

2. Create unrealistic expectations in relationships. Still following the "dream life," you expect perfection from your mate and from yourself. You don't make any room for human error or compromise. You fall for the "seen and not heard" principle, where arguments and truth really don't exist. When you don't live up to or meet society's expectations, you may feel as if you don't measure up. You may feel as if you've missed the mark, or are not a good woman.

The truth of the matter is, much of that is simply bullshit--passive aggressive bullying to convince you that you need these outside forces, characteristics, or accessories to make you feel confident and complete. However, the real truth is that true confidence comes from within. Eventually you start realizing that as a woman, you don't necessarily have to be mild, meek, and quiet. When women speak their minds, or stand up for the things they believe in, they are often described as being aggressive. In actuality, these women are just being assertive.

Additionally, society often teaches you to be passive and avoid who you really are. Heaven forbid you should present yourself authentically. Being authentic means that you don't need the shit that other people bring your way to make you feel confident. Confidence says, "I don't need your color block palette makeup. I don't need your waist cincher. I don't need your positive affirmation. All I need to feel confident is the knowledge that I am beautiful just as I am, and your ass is simply intimidated by my beauty, strength, and intellect. No, I'm not being cocky; I'm being confident!"

Likewise, the media gives us commercials, movies, and songs to influence our way of thinking. By taking their propaganda to heart, a fairytale concept is established in our minds. That fairytale concept eventually becomes our reality.

Society also imposes on us what it feels our jobs should be. You often hear that as a woman, your job is to make a home for your family, be a good woman to your mate, and a good parent to your children. If a woman doesn't do what society believes she should be doing, she will suddenly be deemed a bad parent or mate. In society's eyes, there is no middle ground-- whatever you do is either good or bad. And because you're getting so many messages (drugs) from so many different places, the negative influences soak in, hindering your ability to think reasonably and clearly. That is why people end up living their lives with limitations. Their overall thought process of how to present themselves in relationships is hindered.

3. **Accepting Unacceptable Behavior.** Another pill that society will push on you is the acceptance of unacceptable treatment from a mate. In today's society, women have very low standards when it comes to choosing and accepting negative behavior from a mate. The sad thing is, they think their standards are high when they're actually at an all-time low. But let me be clear, in order for you to set standards, you must embody some yourself!

Some women have been so beat down emotionally, dumbed down intellectually, and cut down physically that they just settle for the first person who comes their way that shows them the least bit of attention. When a friendly suitor comes along, they have convinced themselves through the rhetoric of the world that they have hit a gold mine. For instance, let's say you go on a date with someone. It appears to you that individual seems to be a wonderful person because he or she opens the car door for you, presents you with beautiful flowers, takes you to a nice restaurant, and even pulls out your chair.

Now in the average woman's mind this is a "good catch" because it appears this person has clearly been taught well and knows how to treat a woman. The woman is appreciative and thankful that this person crossed her path. Well, the reality is that the individual's behavior is basic behavior. Opening the car door is not something that goes above and beyond what should be done. Having someone pull out your chair to seat you should be expected when someone takes you out on a date. These acts of kindness should be the standard--your standard.

In the 1940s, 50s, and 60s, it was standard practice for potential mates to show chivalry to the women they were pursuing. Unfortunately, women of today are lowering their standards. Their current expectations from a mate are beneath the standards from years past. As a woman, it is vital that you know what your standards and deal breakers (what you're not willing to compromise about) are.

Another mistake women tend to make is getting overly excited about things that were standard practice 20 years ago. Most women will immediately think that "he or she is the one," This can be described as an impulsive behavior. This occurs when you make quick decisions about relationships, or are "swept away" very easily.

Sadly, some women have no damn clue what their standards are. They base their standards on the opinions of their friends, family members, and society. That's the part that you need to recognize: society is lowering your standards. Remember society is your pusher man. It is pushing pills to you so you can believe that the person that does A, B, and C doesn't exist. However, they do exist. You must patiently wait for them and set your standards. Remember this: your mate will do what he or she wants to do to you, if you allow it. Today, potential and current mates don't have to live up to the expectations that they were once held to years ago. That is why both men and women can get away with doing less and, in some cases, you will still give 110% to the relationship even when it is not being reciprocated.

4. **There Are Not Any Potential Mates Left to Choose From.** One of the biggest pills that society shoves down women's throats is that there are not any potential mates out there. By believing this misconception, a woman will lower (or compromise) her standards to meet someone that's considered by others to be a "good catch." They will try to convince themselves of this by saying, "Well my partner has a good job and provides. They're a good catch. I don't mind if they grab me every now and then. I don't mind if they make me have sex when I don't feel like it. They're a good provider." Sadly, women who think this way don't even recognize these are also levels of abuse. Women swallow all these pills from society and become desperate. They end up getting in unhealthy relationships just so they can say they are 'with' someone. Likewise, women don't hold their partners accountable, but are often very hard on themselves.

Kicking the Habit of Addiction

One of the solutions in kicking the habit of emotional addiction is to first recognize your own self-worth. That's the key. As a woman, you must learn to exert your authority and empower yourself. If you don't recognize your own self-worth, it's not going to work. Secondly, you must understand the strength and power you possess as a woman. This will be an emotional lifestyle change for you. Embrace your uniqueness, body size, and complexion. If you have freckles, embrace them as well. Embrace all those things and see your beauty. Do not look at yourself as needing to be fixed or repaired. You may have things about your body that you don't like, but just because you have those dislikes doesn't mean that you have to accept anything less than respectful treatment from others.

Having a good concept of your self-worth as well as having high self-esteem will prevent you from taking the pusher man's drugs. You will not have to swallow the nonsense if you already know your value. If your belly was already full of the good vitamins and nutrients, you wouldn't have to take what the pusher man offered to you. You would be able to say, "I don't need the pill that you're pushing on the street to make me feel good. I already feel good because I have all my nutrients, which is my mindset and my self-worth." Building a core belief and value system for who you are as a woman, and knowing that you deserve to be treated with respect in every area of your life must be your standard. Never forget that. You have every right to demand respect, unconditional love, and appreciation from another person. These are the things that must be done for you to stop swallowing these pills. You must get on the regimen that's right for you and get yourself internally healthy.

Redefine Your Own Expectations

Every day you are bombarded with negativity. You turn on the news, it's negative. You work with negative people. Hell, gas prices may make you feel negative, right? These constant annoyances that are going on in our lives makes us feel negative, overwhelmed, and stressed out. Often times, there's not a lot of positivity in our lives, because we don't start our day on a positive note.

Most women wake up in the morning and as soon as they hit the alarm button, their brain immediately starts thinking about the things that they must get done and the things that they haven't finished. When you are flooded with unfinished responsibilities, stress comes with it. Because of these conditions, you are unable to recognize the positive aspects of your day, your life, and, most importantly, the positives in you.

Create Your Own Mantra

A mantra is a positive affirmation that you say to yourself every day. It may sound simple, but it will actually have a huge impact on your emotional well-being.

To help you redefine your way of thinking, lessen any existing stress in your life, and strengthen your emotional state of mind, follow these four action steps and write your own mantra.

1. Write It

Grab two sheets of paper. On the first sheet of paper, write down ALL the negative things that you believe about yourself. You're not discounting yourself, but this exercise will add value to your emotional state of mind. Be sure to write everything negative from the way your butt looks, to how you can't seem to conquer a particular task at work. Remember: there's nothing punitive, so whatever negative thoughts you have about yourself, write them ALL down.

2. Flip It

Take all those negative statements that you've made about yourself and turn them into positive statements. Write those on the second sheet of paper. For example, instead of reminding yourself that you haven't lost those five pounds, or that you haven't met an intended deadline, you'll be reading something that says, "My body is a beautiful work of art and a process that's in progress," or, "I may not have achieved everything, but the things that I have done are great." To get out of the negative mindset, you must start surrounding yourself with positivity--both through your mantra as well as with positive people.

3. Post It

After you have written all your positive affirmations, post your mantra in a place where you will be able to see it-- preferably on your bathroom mirror.

4. Read It

On a daily basis, as soon as you get up in the morning and before you go to bed at night, read the positive affirmations out loud. Get used to hearing your voice speak positively. Get used to hearing positive things about yourself. This routine will eventually become your new way of thinking.

Recognize and Surround Yourself with Positive People

Every person who asks you, "How's your day?" doesn't really want good news. You must be able to recognize who the positive individuals are. These are the people in your life who not only support you when things are going well, but also call you out when you're not doing what you're supposed to be doing. They support you through the entire process and are not those "fly by night" people who only swoop in when you're experiencing trauma, hurt, pain, and disappointment. Those fair-weather people have all the advice in the world, but you can't find them when you really need them the most. Your positive circle is a small carefully-selected crew of individuals who are always there whether you're up or down. These are people that have been steadfast and loyal to you. They always give it to you straight. These are the people that sometimes annoy you because you don't always want to hear their honest criticism. Most of the time, however, what they are saying about your situation is the truth. These are the types of positive people that you need in your life.

Sometimes, before positive people can come into your life,

you must first make the conscious decision to purge the negative people from your life, including family. If family members end up being your drug of choice, meaning that you are depending on family to provide your emotional stability and happiness, that dynamic can be just as addictive. You must purge yourself of those negative individuals as well. Do not rationalize their presence in your life because they are family. It's not okay that they bring you down, or only call you when they need something. It's not okay that they transfer their responsibility to you and, all of a sudden, make it your job to do this or that for them. Those are some of the things that you must recognize in yourself and in the circle around you-- family or not. Doing so will help you start to build a more positive concept of self-worth. You must reframe the way you think, evaluating your environment and asking yourself, "How often are these people there when I need them or when I'm down? Can I lean on them? Can I turn my switch from on to off and count on them to still be there?" You must ask yourself those hard questions. In answering those questions honestly, you can begin the process of saying "No" to others and "Yes" to yourself.

Reflections
Step 2
Society is Your Pusher Man

_____

_____

_____

_____

_____

_____

_____

_____

_____

_____

_____

_____

_____

_____

_____

_____

_____

_____

_____

_____

_____

_____

STEP 3

GATEWAY **EMOTIONS** AND **TRIGGERS**

*I*n this section, you will learn several truths about emotional addiction, which run parallel to substance abuse addiction. Each parallel will paint a vivid picture of what triggers an addicted person.

Your sight, smell, taste, touch, and hearing senses all play a significant role in emotional addiction. They all become triggers for your emotional cycle. These triggers are often reasons why you need to pass up the relationship, or why you often bring previous emotions into new relationships. The key is to recognize what your triggers are and to create effective methods of coping with and dissolving them so that they do not continue to have a long-standing impact on the rest of your life.

NOTE: The senses outlined below are focused on physical abuse, but they also can be applied to emotional addiction with a little manipulation of perception.

You may have loved someone who is a drug addict. One moment they are living the clean life, free of drugs, and the next moment they have relapsed. As with any addiction, the vicious cycle of seeing a loved one's life in constant flux is heartbreaking. There may even have been times in which you wondered, "Why do they keep relapsing and going back to that same destructive pattern? They just can't seem to stay clean. What is the deal with them?"

Gateway #1: Sense of Smell

Oftentimes we treat the drug of choice, but we don't treat the senses that are associated with the drug. Those senses are the triggers, which keep the addiction growing. For example, let's say a drug user smokes crack in a house that's located next to a KFC restaurant. While they are engaging in their drug use, they are smelling the aroma of the food from KFC. Let's also assume that there's a fire station down the street. The drug user hears sirens going off while consuming drugs. Visually, the user will associate colors similar to red and burgundy with whatever drugs they are consuming, as those are the colors of both KFC and fire stations. From the sound of sirens to the smell of grease and colors in varying shades of red, a number of the senses are being activated during consumption.

Now, let's say the individual goes to a rehab near a beach in California. They no longer have access to drugs and do not have to focus on negative influences. Their family members are thinking, "Okay, now they're good."

If the former abuser comes back home clean (no longer using drugs), what causes them to have a relapse? They relapse because the aroma of KFC is a trigger that reminds them of past drug use. They relapse when they hear sirens. They even relapse when they see the color red or burgundy. These are factors that some therapeutic programs don't consider.

Relationships often have some of the very same relapse characteristics.

One of the things that is a huge trigger for women is their sense of smell. Although you may have dissolved a relationship with a mate, when you smell the cologne or perfume your former partner used to wear, that trigger often brings back emotions. Those emotions could be either romantic, or painful. Therefore, when you recognize the scent on any other potential mate, there is an automatic emotional withdrawal from or push towards the relationship. It may also be that you fall back into past relationships because you are romantically drawn to the scent and feel a sense of comfort and security around those who wear it.

This process is a lot like when you smell your grandmother's home cooking. That smell is the trigger, which makes you think back to how it made you feel to be cooking in the kitchen with her or spending holidays together. Such triggers are why you may keep falling back into the same relationships or falling into similar relationships with other people. The sense of smell boosts our memory and triggers mental pictures that remind us of past times. Smelling the cologne or perfume in an environment, you now find that you're mentally back in a place where a past mate aroused you. It's at that very moment that your brain thinks, "Aww man, I wish I could go back there just for a split second". Without recognizing it, you just opened a gateway for a possible relapse to occur.

Gateway #2: Sense of Sound

Every person has a soundtrack for their lives. If you think back to the pivotal points that you've experienced throughout your life, there's a song that goes along with each moment.

You may be driving in your car when suddenly that song comes on the radio. While listening to the song, your mind retreats to the past. You're no longer listening to the words of the song. Instead you're thinking about that good time or that pleasant feeling you experienced. Whatever the emotion is that you feel, it is the very thing that connects you to the song. So, the sense of sound ends up being another gateway that causes you to start craving that old feeling again.

Gateway #3: Sense of Sight

Oftentimes, women will try to purge themselves of a relationship. They do the whole out of sight, out of mind thing. That crap does not work, at all. All that does is prolong the inevitable. Women tell themselves, "Okay, I won't look at that person. I won't look at their Facebook. I'll block them." They go through this whole blocking phase, blocking phones and computers. They delete pictures and get rid of physical stuff. However, they refuse to purge the emotional baggage. They talk themselves into believing, "Well, they're not here, so I don't have to think about them. I'm not going to be triggered by them. I'm going to move on." However, when you run into your former mate on the street, your whole world crashes because you didn't take the time to heal emotionally. When you see them or objects that remind you of them, it brings back memories. If the person that you dated was an avid Prince fan or an avid collector of shot glasses, when you see shot glasses or hear an old Prince song, you experience an automatic trigger because you haven't undergone the necessary internal purging or healing.

Gateway #4: Sense of Touch

Touch also plays a role because our skin is one of the largest sense organs that we have on our body and is the source of all of our feelings. Because women are known to use the right side (the emotional side) of their brains more than the left, women tend to be associated more with emotions, feelings, senses, and vibes than men. The sense of touch is often a trigger that can be either positive or negative.

Let's say you were physically abused in the past and someone touches or grabs you in the same place as your abuser. That would be a negative trigger. Now think about the "feel good" touch. As you probably have already guessed, a "feel good" touch is a positive trigger. Let's say you're out on a date with someone and you tell yourself that you're going to take it slow. If you have not dealt with old feelings from past relationships and your new mate happens to give you a slight pinch on the arm or hold your hand in a way that reminds you of past relationships, they may have unknowingly awakened your past emotions. Sometimes those old, romantic feelings that you had from previous relationships will transfer to your next mate whom you've only been dating for a week. So, because you only healed yourself externally, but forgot about your internal wounds, you're now experiencing all this transferring of feelings simply because he or she hit a physical trigger point that you were not even aware of.

Gateway #5: Sense of Taste

The sense of taste can be a huge trigger when enjoying quality time with your mate. This consists of having meals and sharing recipes together. Dating consists of a lot of dinners. The restaurants and the taste of the food often take you to a place where you felt very happy. In the end, you get an emotional rush from the meal and apply those feelings to the person that you're currently having the meal with. This is how these senses can trigger your emotional cravings.

There are all kinds of triggers that can cause you to fall back into the same cycle of unhealthy relationships. As soon as you stop moving forward and start reverting back to your past, the sense of security that you once found in past relationships has you bound all over again.

Forgiveness of Self

Forgiveness is not about other people, forgiveness is about you. When you forgive, you are forgiving the fact that you have allowed yourself to be controlled emotionally by another person. Even though that person has passed away or moved on with their lives, you're still carrying the emotional baggage from that trauma. In order for you to move on with your life, you must forgive yourself for holding onto the pain. Tell yourself, "I release myself from the trauma. It's my turn to heal. I'm going to live in the now and that is a choice that I must make. But first I must recognize the trauma." In order to get past the heaviness of the pain, this process really does take seeking some type of therapy. Though the process may involve minor setbacks, rest reassured that your setbacks are just set ups for your come-back! It's necessary for you to break the wall down that you've built in order for you to reconstruct it with a stronger foundation.

Building Your Self-Esteem and Learning to Say Yes to Yourself

Now that you know the backdrop of your past experiences and emotions, let's focus more on your health. Be proud of who you've become thus far in your life. The mantra that you've created will become even more powerful. When you first create your mantra, there's still some underlying baggage. The meaning is great, but it's only a short-term fix. It simply helps you get to the good phase of your life by providing you the positivity that you need. Once you begin to get past your trauma and identify your realistic expectations, then and only then will you be able to live for today. When you do, you will be able to start saying, "Yes" to yourself, which means saying, "No" to others." I use that quote often with my clients, students, and myself. Sometimes you must say "No" to others and say "Yes" to yourself. Sometimes you must be selfish instead of selfless. Sometimes you must invest in yourself.

Women often feel guilty when they choose to say "No" in order to invest in themselves. So, what women tend to do is accept less but give more. We'll say, "Yes" to making someone else's needs a priority while our needs aren't being met. If you continue to do that, you end up falling further and further behind. Now is the time for you to say "No" to others and "Yes" to yourself. Individuals who generally have your back and unconditionally love you will be totally okay with you saying "No" to them. Why? Because they recognize that now it's time for your growth and will support you in your growth. They will even ask, "What can I do to help you?"

Also during this time, you will begin to notice people leaving you. Trust and believe that their departure is a good thing. When you start living in the now—saying "yes" to yourself-- all the naysayers, doubters, and people that were only happy to be there when you were willing to say "Yes" for them will fall off. This is the season in your life in which you will find yourself shedding your old emotions, connections, and fears. All of your old emotional skin will just fall off and the people that are attached to it will fall off, too. You'll begin to feel a little lighter. You'll walk with your head higher. Your steps will be...well, you'll be damn-near gliding at this point, because you have shed all the weight from your life. Your phone may not ring as much, but you'll be in a happier place. Besides, you were tired of answering the phone anyway. All these positive things will take place by you saying one word to yourself: "Yes!" Your core crew may get a little bit smaller, but those remaining are the key relationships that you need to love and nurture the most.

Being Single Does Not Mean You're Alone

As mentioned earlier, there is a difference from being single versus being lonely. Just because you're single doesn't mean you're alone.

Stop right now and meditate for a moment.

Now look around you.

You have all these things in your life that you have built up for yourself. You've added quality to your life. You recognize that you are complete without a mate.

Have you ever watched a movie where the person who's in the relationship tells their partner, "You complete me?" The truth is that they don't. In real life, the problems an individual has when he or she enters a relationship will more than likely be the same problems when he or she exits the relationship. And the happiness had when entering the relationship will be (or should be) the same (if not more) happiness, when exiting the relationship.

A mate is an extension of your life; they're not the absolute value of your life. My husband is one of my best accessories. He's like red bottom shoes or a handpicked diamond bracelet. He's an extension of and a complement to my greatness. Although I'm great as an individual, my husband accessorizes my greatness. And I know I am an accessory to him. Being complete is when you recognize that you can absolutely live without your partner. You can breathe, walk, talk, eat and do a number of other things without that person. That's what makes you strong. That's what makes you assertive. Independence is what makes you great, but you'd rather not live without your partner. I can totally live without my husband, and my husband can live without me, but we would rather not. That's the difference.

Focus on the Best You

When you recognize that you:

1. Have people in your circle who are supportive;

2. Don't need a relationship to feel complete; and

3. Now have time to focus on yourself as an individual to build your legacy, brand, and complete your desired goals, then you're focusing on the best you!

Once you start focusing on the best you, your ideal mate will show up. From there, everything else will flow much more naturally.

Reflections
Step 3
Gateway Emotions and Triggers

_____

_____

_____

_____

_____

_____

_____

_____

_____

_____

_____

_____

_____

_____

_____

_____

_____

_____

_____

_____

_____

STEP 4

FAULTY CONSUMPTION AND **SYMPTOMS**

*L*et's face it: we are suckers for love. Almost every little girl has pretended to be a bride. We played house and pretended to be mommies and daddies as children. For some, it is so engrained in their minds to desire their very own Prince Charming who will come rescue them from the evil in the world. From Disney to Lifetime, the media has given us a misconstrued representation of love, romance, and healthy relationships.

We want to believe that our relationships WILL lead to marriage. We are confident that we have what it takes to transform our mates into individuals who "walk on sunshine" every time they think about us. Yes, our husbands or wives will "pay our rent and be faithful lovers, as soon as they get home from work". Our woman power causes us to believe that there will never be an "end of the road" and that if we just push a little harder, sacrifice a little more, and sweep things under the rug, we will always have a "house that is a home".

Our identity, our purpose, our souls depend on it, right?

Wrong!

Because of this incorrect mindset, women tend to ignore red flags. We sacrifice our needs because we so desperately want to be saved. Our 30's have come and, for some of us, have gone without a ring. We no longer want to be a single lady begging him or her to put a ring on it! Give us the ring already! According to society, the ring symbolizes completion. Someone decided that he or she wanted you for the rest of their life, and if you haven't received a ring yet, something must be personally wrong.

Women can be so desperate for a rock on their finger that they settle. Instead of facing the reality of their mate's personality and character traits, they focus on the potential!

The "P" Word

Promises?
No!
Passion?
Not quite!
Potential?
You got it!

Potential: Our downfall, our muse, our worst distraction, our rhythm and blues.

Women who place too much value on the ring and fairy tales, can find themselves falling in love with a mate's potential instead of his or her truth. They fantasize about them getting the perfect job and living in the house with a white picket fence and 2.5 kids. In reality though, they find themselves cohabitating with someone who refuses to go to work, is dishonest and emotionally-challenged, and who has to borrow someone else's vehicle due to not having one of their own. This tainted mindset is an initial symptom of emotional addiction.

Accepting the reality of our mates, prevents us from unnecessary heartache and heartbreak. It also saves time. When a woman focuses solely on the potential instead of the truth, she tends to invest more time into the relationship than she should. Instead of looking at the red flags and honoring her deal-breakers, she puts her emotional and mental state in harm's way.

Good Sex, Bad Relationships

Let's talk about the good ole orgasm. Sometimes it becomes such an "ultimate goal" during an intimate encounter that it can blind our good judgement.

Meet Tracey.
26 years old; Heterosexual; Educated; Divorced; and a mother of 2.
She was an educator and used to have a stable career.
She had her own place and car and paid her own bills.

Despite the failure of her marriage, she bounced back and focused on making sure her children had what they needed. She refused to let a man dictate the quality of her livelihood. Her determination and drive proved she would be alright.

And she was... until she met Michael.
Hardworking.
Family-oriented. Dedicated.
Gorgeous.

Tracey fell quick.
But there were signs everywhere.

He wasn't emotionally connected to her. He could go days without talking to her, yet she continued to chase him. "Some" time was better than no time in her eyes. Her love language was words of affirmation and quality time, but Michael never filled up her love tank with sweet words, encouragement, or appreciation. His time with her was inconsistent.

They argued so much that friends and family members would make comments.

No matter how much Tracey would cry and make the decision to release herself from Michael, she couldn't go through with it.

Why?

He gave her some good sex. Every time they broke up, he knew he could get her back with sex. The yearning to be touched, to feel needed, though temporary, was a high for her. When she came down, his truth was still there but the orgasm gave her a little more strength to stay connected.

Orgasms are powerful, but they are misleading. Those few seconds of ecstasy shouldn't affect our decision-making. Unfortunately for Tracey, it did. She continued to stay with Michael, believing that he would live up to the expectations that were in her mind. They eventually married. Fast-forward 10 years, Tracey is disappointed with her marriage and suffering from depression and anxiety. She has lost hope that things will change, and continues to stay in her marriage for the sake of convenience.

Internally, Tracey wishes she would have accepted the truth 10 years ago, and paid more attention to the red flags instead of basing her future on a man's ability to give her a few moments of pleasure.

Because Tracey overlooked the red flags in her relationship with Michael, she is saying, "My emotional self and my spiritual self are not worth it." This couldn't be further from the truth. We are not just sexual objects. We are powerful. We are beautiful. We are purposely flawed. We are perfectly imperfect. We're spiritual beings. We're the essence of life.

If we are so many wonderful things, why do so many of us carry ourselves like sex objects? There are many reasons. Our culture, the media, and the music we listen to all play a role in how we carry ourselves in relationships. But ultimately, it's still your decision.

Depending on your culture, you may have been taught that the way to a man's heart is dictated by how you cook and put it on him in the bedroom.

We hear songs about it. A lot of our music and media that we consume is loaded with sexual connotations and innuendos. Sex sells. We're constantly being bombarded with these sexual signals. The sexual experience is no longer sacred. It is everywhere. We fall into the trap of focusing on our sexual lives instead of our emotional and mental wellbeing.

Instead of taking our One-A-Day vitamin that help us spiritually, emotionally, and physically, we choose to pop this "quickie" pill. Hopefully, in return, feelings of sexual beauty will blossom and our identity will be established in the eyes of our mates. "Yes, sex is the answer," we tell our minds. We say it so much that we continue to stay in broken relationships, just like Tracey, hoping that they will turn around. They must because the sex is just that good! What a faulty consumption!

Sexual Addiction

Now you're probably thinking to yourself, "But Dr. East, it is so good! I don't know how to stop."

You may not realize it but you have fallen into the trap of sexual addiction. You are sexually addicted to someone when you become physically attached and are unable to enforce standards, expectations, or boundaries.

Some women find themselves engaging in numerous one-night stands, or booty calls. They may constantly feel the need to be in bed with someone because that is how they define acceptance or an emotional connection with another person. In reality, this is only temporary gratification and doesn't touch the root of the issue. It only becomes a quick fix for a recurring problem.

During sex, chemicals are released that cause us to crave what a person can do to us physically more than emotionally or spiritually. During sex, those other factors of our lives aren't as important. Sex becomes our drug of choice. Raheem Devaughn's song, "Love Drug" talks about this. We become "lovaholics" for each other even though love isn't anywhere in the equation. It's just sex. Once the physical attachment is made, we believe that we can make a broken relationship work. We become fiends for each other, and can't function unless reconnection occurs.

If you are struggling with this, like Tracey, you are a sex addict, honey!

Reflections
Step 4
Faulty Consumption & Symptoms

TOXIC THOUGHTS:
THE DISEASE TO PLEASE

*F*or some reason, it is extremely hard for us as a female species to put ourselves "first." If you are like me, you probably grew up in a household where your mom was superwoman. She worked a full-time job, came home to cook, clean, and take care of her man and children. She was the first person to get up in the morning and more than likely, the last one to go to bed at night. Mama was the backbone of the house. She sacrificed, sacrificed, and sacrificed some more. It was her responsibility.

How many of you find yourself in the same role?

Let's keep it real! It is perfectly okay to take care of your family and your household. There is nothing wrong with sacrificing things at times, but you were not created to just be a wife and mother!

What about you? What about what you need? When was the last time that you thought about your goals, dreams, and aspirations?

Society and our mates over the years have caused us to believe that putting ourselves first is selfish. There isn't any room for self-indulging behavior. There are too many dishes in the sink; clothes need ironing; baby girl has a project due this week. How dare we take a nightly bubble bath, get a mani/pedi, or take a weekend road trip with our girlfriends.

There is just too much work to do!

We are all Super Woman, remember?

We can't blame it all on society or even our mates, either. Many women won't take the time to pamper themselves because they are sick with the disease to please.

What will they think if you don't put the laundry away before they come home? Won't the kids starve if dinner isn't made immediately?

For some women, serving their partners and children makes them feel better about themselves. Without it they are lost.

Though women tend to be the nurturers, healers, and rescuers in their homes, there's much more to who we are. You must see yourself through a larger lens than the narrative that society has crafted.

What good are you if you are constantly being the nurturer, healer, and rescuer, but never replenish what you have poured out? No matter what your mother or grandmother may have been capable of, failure to take time out for yourself will not make you more effective.

At times, being selfish is necessary, honey!

You know what else is necessary?

Your ability to say "No."

Saying "No" helps you decide what fits in your life. It is okay to say "No" to that relationship that is killing you emotionally. It is perfectly fine to want more, to release things that have held you captive, and to let go so that you can be free emotionally, spiritually, and physically.

There is also a misconception that if you are a certain age you should already have a spouse, home, and 2.5 kids. I remember being thirty and having to remind individuals that I was still a real woman even though I wasn't married and didn't have a child. I wasn't missing out, I was successful and happy. Women shouldn't allow this fear of not meeting certain deadlines established by society to dictate how they live and transition through life.

You are not a failure if you are still single. You are not a failure if your mate is unhappy. You are not a failure if things are falling apart in your household. One or more factors contribute to the failure of any situation. You're not fully responsible. So, release those toxic thoughts because they force us into being more concerned with making everyone else happy while denying ourselves pleasure.

At the end of the day, you are the most important person in your life.

You must get over people pleasing and focus more on "me" pleasing! If you are not happy with your life, you should NOT be focusing on helping make someone else happy.

If you are not okay with something, the people who truly love you should not be okay either.

Another toxic thought that creeps into the minds of many women is the notion of comparison. Your relationship could be extremely detrimental to your wellbeing, but compared to your best friend's situation, you may actually be in pretty good shape. Unfortunately, that kind of comparison is a form of bondage.

By rationalizing staying in a broken relationship because it isn't as bad as the ones on T.V., or those of others around you, you're placing yourself in shackles. Although your relationship isn't healthy, you make excuses and stick it out because, on the surface, it seems better than theirs.

Whose life are you living? Remember: you are the most important person in your life and what you need matters.

So, how do I change these toxic thoughts? I am glad you asked!

You replace the negative thoughts with positive ones and reframe them. Reframing is critical.

When you reframe, you take a negative situation and find the brighter side in it. This, my friend, will take a lot of work, but it can be done. In order to be optimistic instead of pessimistic, you may need to disconnect from what's around you. It is now all about choosing the positive life.

You must also remember that you can only control your own actions. It isn't your responsibility to fix everybody in your circle. It isn't going to happen. Write down all the things that you do in your life that you feel are your responsibility. Once these things are written, go down the list and assess whether these items are really your responsibility. Are you the sole person responsible, or can someone else get it done?

After you have gone down your list, I promise that you will realize that you are taking on responsibilities that you shouldn't have to shoulder alone.

There are some things in life that are just out of your control, and that, can be a hard pill to swallow. You are in control of you. You control how you act, no matter the situation. You can control your responses, your thoughts, your movements, and more. Women are powerful. We control how we lead our lives.

Once you understand what you control, you will have a better handle on how the behaviors of others affect you. You will not feel personally attacked if someone doesn't rise to the level of your expectations, or doesn't follow through. Again, you are not in control of their actions.

Being positive and controlling toxic thoughts takes practice. You can do it! Find something positive in everything that you do. Think about the lessons that you have learned from an unfavorable situation. How can you grow to make yourself an even better woman?

Once you have established these principles and systems in your life, you can apply them and live happily no matter what comes your way.

Reflections
Step 5
Toxic Thoughts: The Disease to Please

STEP 6

WITHDRAWAL

*W*omen are such beautiful creatures. Our hair, our skin, our style, our walk-- all of it is amazing. Not only are we beautiful, but we are also great pretenders. We know how to mask our pain well. A woman can be heartbroken but will beat her face with the latest MAC foundation, eye shadow, lashes, and more, and you would never know. She could be emotionally distraught, but will show up to work and/or church with the most expensive outfit and shoes. Focusing on her outward appearance becomes a coping mechanism. Instead of dealing with the internal dilemmas, the emotional addictions, or toxic mindsets, she goes to the gym to work off the dozen donuts she ate the night before to make her feel better. Unfortunately, true change doesn't happen unless it occurs within, and it doesn't happen overnight.

Deep Change vs. Surface Change

Women put on for the world because we don't want to show any crevices or cracks. However, it's through those cracks that the light shines. If there weren't cracks in dark places, there would be no light. If there weren't any holes in tunnels, there wouldn't be any way through them. The cracks and holes are what we use to light the path to our new destinations; our best selves.

When we start talking about deep changes, we're talking about inner change--that spiritual change of knowing your worth and your value. I don't mean religion. That's not our focus. When I say spiritual, I want you to focus on your worth and value as a woman--your spirit of strength, possibilities, capabilities, and accomplishments. Go past the surface and tap into your own self-worth. For many, this is one of the hardest things to do.

We will get cosmetic surgery and surround ourselves with friends that aren't as cute, but all of these things are superficial and do not add to our internal growth as women.

Progress Not Perfection

Another mistake we make is that we focus on perfection and never make it through the progress phase. There are steps you must take to achieve all that you want in life as well as setbacks and struggles that you must endure. Remember: setbacks are nothing but set ups for a comeback.

Many times, we look at the process of working and progressing and want immediate results. Why? Because society says it's possible. Many women have the "Burger King" mentality: we want it our way. We have to have it fast and right now. Society has trained us to microwave every situation, relationship, and career. The quicker it comes, the better it is. We get things delivered to our house because we don't want to wait in line. We don't want to cook meals, so we order things that are already prepared. We ascribe to a quick-fix mentality in our lives where if we don't want to work out, we take supplements or drink a shake instead. This isn't the way to reach goals, though.

Anything that lasts and has substance takes some crawling, fighting, and digging to earn. We focus on quick fixes so much and withdraw when it doesn't happen on our time.

We go through withdrawal symptoms in our relationships. We withdraw because we don't like that feeling of loneliness that turns into fear. The fear then turns to anxiety of questioning whether we're ever going to be in a positive relationship. We start questioning whether the right person even exists.

When we withdraw, we sometimes begin to fall back into old behavior. We need to realize that progress is in small steps. Even the smallest of steps can lead to the greatest outcomes. We must recognize that every measure that we take towards a goal of healing internally is a step closer to us being our true selves. That road is not supposed to be quick, easy, or perfect. If it were, we wouldn't appreciate it once we got to the finish line.

Growing Through the Pain

Oftentimes, as women, we want to avoid the pain of the breakup, being single, or, as I call it, feeling alone. We want to avoid those pains so much that we distract ourselves with projects and other people. We can grow through that pain. If you cut yourself, it hurts. But if you put ointment on it and allow it to breathe, it will heal. It may still bother you if you aggravate it, but through the pain, there will be growth.   We grow through the same process when dealing with our emotional addictions.   You must grow through that feeling of being hurt.

We may not understand the process at the time, but it serves as a painful reminder of what we want to avoid experiencing again.   During the pain, it's important that we ask ourselves, "What am I going to do next time that's going to be different? How can I make sure that I do not go through this pain again?"

When we grow through the pain that we experience, we allow ourselves to apply life lessons of value and substance that can carry us forward. We have a better visual concept of what a healthy relationship looks like. And honey, that is the beginning of your healing.

Healing in any way, shape, form, or fashion never starts pleasurably. There's always a sense of anger, sadness, or physical pain. But we heal.

Do you know what else we do? We become more versatile. We become more agile, and the inner-emotional strength propels us to survive difficult relationships. Applying our newly-acquired knowledge, we are able to embrace new relationships with different eyes.

We tend to forget that there is more than one road that we can travel to get to our destination. As human beings, we sometimes have tunnel vision. We see the finish line and say, "this is the way that we're going to get there." No matter an individual's belief system, there are auras and vibes, that guide us to where we need to be. It is important to recognize that just because there may be a roadblock, it doesn't mean that there isn't another route you can take.

When going through processes, struggles, and challenges, think of this metaphor: while walking down the street, you find a boulder in your way. Since there's only one road, some people get to the boulder and say, "You know what, I'm just going to turn around and not go." Those people don't want to do the work of having to chisel through. The thing is, if you can chisel through the rock and make it through to the other side, when you come back, you're not going to have as much work to do. In the end, that road becomes much easier to travel.

Every time we start to work on those flaws and chisel away slowly at things that are causing us discomfort, it makes it easier to talk about. We can live despite our hardships, and can transform the lives of others through our testimonies. We all go through difficult stretches. The important thing is to recognize that these phases aren't flaws; they're just a piece of who we are.

It is important for you to recognize the specific signs of your falling into a state of withdrawal. The first sign occurs when we seclude ourselves. We go into hiding and stop engaging in social activities because we have a hard time being in social settings where other people are happy.

We don't understand why this is. It could, for example, be separation from a best friend. We should be happy for their successes, but we have this underlying feeling of frustration, anger, or jealousy.

Another sign shows up when we start to make excuses. Sometimes we make excuses for why we don't have time to do something, saying "well, you know I don't have the energy to invest in that," or, "I don't have the time to invest in that." Those are all excuses that we make so that we can avoid doing the work.

You may also notice withdrawal symptoms when you fall back into unhealthy behavior patterns that you were recently working on healing. You'll find yourself falling back in old behaviors or habits, rather than sticking with the process. You'll give up your daily meditation and weekly bubble baths because those things become less of a priority for you. When you stop putting energy into the things that made you a better you, you're falling into the trap of withdrawal.

Reflections
Step 6
Withdrawal

JUST ONE MORE HIT:
Emotional Relapse

Quick Fix: Are You Self-Medicating?

Letting go is difficult. Starting over can be equally frustrating at times. What do you do when you find yourself emotionally relapsing? Are you self-medicating to function daily? When people self-medicate, they put things into place that keep them from facing the emotions and feelings of the pain of withdrawal.

This transition is tough, isn't it?

Trust me, I get it.

I can imagine the wheels turning in your brain, trying to figure out what "quick fix" you can put in place to help you get by. The emotional pain is kicking your butt, and you're desperately trying to figure out a solution to numb the beatings.

Here are some ineffective quick fixes:

• Becoming a serial dater or joining the online dating scene;

• Going in and out of the new hot spots in town;

• Shopping for new outfits to look the part of "having it all together;"

• Void-filling

Here is the problem: You have not had any time to yourself.

You haven't given yourself time to grieve and heal. These quick fixes that you have put in place to numb your emotional pain will eventually wear off. You are still addicted to your original drug of choice: your emotional attachment. Your series of dates, shopping trips, and jumping from one party to another will not measure up to the quality of the emotional high you received from your original drug.

You may find yourself stuck, trying to replace that feeling of bliss, and losing all at the same time. If you have added a new sexual encounter, you again find yourself in an emotional bind.

When we use one-night stands and sex as quick fixes, we refuse to truly acknowledge and deal with the addiction, and the cycle continues. We rationalize by telling ourselves, "This person isn't for me. They didn't have that spark." Worse still, we try to compare the new person with the one that gets us emotionally high.

We sabotage relationships and waste time with individuals that we don't want because we're afraid of going through the withdrawals that we discussed in Chapter 6.

Who wants to go through the process of feeling alone, sad, and used? No one. Even though it is a necessary part of the process, the fact that it's unpleasant may cause you to replace your feelings with unfulfilling relationships, knowing that you aren't ready to commit to anyone new.

 In doing so, you are affecting your new mate's self-worth without even realizing it through your lack of commitment. As a result, that person doesn't get introduced to family and friends because you're "just kicking it." In your eyes, they're just someone you are seeing to help you get over your emotional pain.

Honey, this will get old and can create further damage.

One of the hardest but most important things to do is to sit still. I know that you may have a fear of being alone, but being alone does not equate to being lonely. Even without a significant other, you are not lonely. Instead of serial dating, when was the last time that you invested in yourself? There are other things in life that are fulfilling other than being in a relationship. What about your family, friends (outside of social media), career, and health? These are things that are just as important.

Stop and take time for yourself. Get off of social media and dating sites. Not forever, but until you're ready. I get that social dating sites inspire hope for the common working woman to meet someone, especially when she is busy. But when you start to use these services as vices, you are almost abusing the system. Stop swiping for dates and start dating yourself!

When was the last time that you took a long, hot bath or even took yourself out to the movies? It is okay to take yourself out for a picnic or head to the beach to reflect. When was the last time that you pampered yourself?

As women, we sometimes forget to invest time in ourselves. What are your interests? Think about them and cultivate those gifts.

If you want to be a better cook, then take a cooking class. Watch cooking shows on T.V. and try out a new recipe every week. Share what you've made with your friends, allowing those individuals to fill the spaces that you need filled without getting into the sexual, physical, and emotional transference of people over and over again.

The Cover Up

Are you ok?

Not really.

But are you ready to reveal your true condition? Most women aren't.

Earlier we discussed how we want others to think that we are perfectly happy. Everything is normal. Our past relationship may have broken us, but we don't want the world to know that.

Many women are afraid that their authenticity will be judged. So instead of embracing their current place, they cover it up with makeup, jewelry, expensive cars, and more. They refuse to reveal their withdrawal symptoms to the world.

No, we can't show that we're missing our ex. Everything must seem normal. We're good. Our communication with people in our circle never addresses the past relationship or our current emotional health. We talk about jobs, T.V., or current events, but are not willing to dive deep into relationship talk. Instead of connecting, we deflect.

In our minds, we will be judged if we tell the truth. We've been raised to believe that it is our job to maintain the relationship. We were told that women are the ones that keep the home happy. We are responsible for the sexiness in our relationships. What will our friends think if we talk about how broken our relationship is? The biggest fear is that our inner circle will find out that we have flaws.

The reality is that our inner circles are supposed to be our "crew." They are people we can be real around. These are individuals that we can trust. We should be able to be most vulnerable around them. However, because of the pressures that we put on ourselves to be strong, independent, and not needy, we feel the need to put up facades around them. Instead of allowing ourselves to heal in our safe place around the people we're supposed to be able to trust, we cover up our scars and pretend that everything is fine. Unfortunately, when we get home, we park our cars, take off the makeup, unzip the costume, and are stuck with ourselves, in our own spaces.

Emotional relapse occurs because we have not been given an opportunity to be real. The faking it until we make it doesn't last long. Eventually we fall off and retreat back to our emotional addiction, or find someone with similar characteristics to feed our need.

Let's go back to Step 2 for a moment and expand on how to create your mantra. This is going to sound odd, but it's something that I have my female clients do when they're having difficulties embracing themselves. I ask them to strip completely naked and stare in the mirror. I'm not there, of course. I then tell them, "I want you to write down all the things you don't like about yourself, the things that annoy you, even the little things you may not like, such as the spreading of your hips or your feet." You may not like that mole on the side of your face, your stretch marks, or any number of other imperfections.

Whatever the flaw, women can find a million, right? Pick out the things that you don't like. Then either on your own or with a professional, flip those dislikes. Turn those negatives into positives. Instead of saying, "My hips are so wide," change that platform and say, "my hips occupy the spaces that are needed for growth," or "my hips provide the curves that represent my femininity." All of a sudden, your hips don't look so bad.

Let's say you had a kid and now you have stretch marks--a thing most women complain about. Instead of saying, "I hate my stretch marks," say, "my stretch marks are signs of bringing life into the world. My stretch marks represent the beautiful creations that I have. My stretch marks represent the obstacles that I've faced and overcome in my life." Replace "I hate the bags underneath my eyes," with "the bags underneath my eyes represent the hard work and dedication that I put in every day."

You get the idea? You're taking all of those negative things about yourself and flipping them into positive attributes.

Your mantra is you. You can look them up online, but I like them to be very personal. Because if we wake up every day and read our mantra, we're waking up every day to something positive. It's very easy to wake up negative. We've been taught to wake up to negativity, but when we wake up every day to something positive, we're able to reflect on ourselves and our bodies, and that motivates us. We're starting off our day with a good head on our shoulders that's full of positive energy. We must recognize that jewelry, cars, jobs, and makeup are just accessories. We're absolutely flawless and beautiful. We're perfect in spite of our imperfections.

Confusing a Need with a Want

Do we really know what we need? Emotional relapse occurs because we are trying to fulfill a need. Did that emotional addiction truly give us what we needed?

As women, sometimes, we can confuse a need with a want. We tend to be delusional when it comes to the two.

I often ask women in therapy sessions, what are your deal-breakers and what is it that you need? In most cases, they give me a long list of their wants, albeit unintentionally.

I'll say, "What is it that you need from a significant other?"

"Well, I want them to make money and respect me."

I reply, "I didn't ask what you wanted, what is it that you need?"

What do you need as a woman to feel that a mate is a positive addition to your life? Many times women aren't able to come up with an answer. They aren't sure what they need and tend to focus on materialistic items. They tend not to say, "I need someone to take care of me when I'm sick," or "I need someone to show sympathy for me when I'm having a rough day." These are foundational principles that every woman should want in their relationships. These characteristics make us feel safe and secure.

Confusing a need with a want reflects an unclear understanding of what you need in your relationship. Instead, you become consumed with what they can offer now rather than what they can provide you long-term.

Some women are just excited about being in a relationship and are in love with the idea of being "in love." Some women are just happy that they are no longer single-- grateful that they have someone to take them out or travel with. These roles don't fill a need but a want. Wants are short-term. Any relationship that solely fulfills our wants instead of needs are considered quick fixes. Instead of taking the time to internally heal and feel complete on our own, we connect to individuals hoping to feel okay. These quick fixes set women up for continuous emotional relapse.

We should get to the core of our value systems and beliefs. What do we value the most in a person beyond anything else? For me, honesty, work ethic, and morals are three of the core values I look for in another. Notice I didn't say, "white collar, six figures," or "showers me with gifts," because those aren't my core values. I can shower myself with gifts and make six figures on my own. That is not what I need from my mate. I need my mate to be a hard worker. If I know my mate is a hard worker, no matter what task is put before him, he's going to give it 110%.

Whether it's being a mate to me, being a parent for our child, or supporting the household in the decisions that we need to make, I find comfort in hard work and honesty. When shit hits the fan, society becomes jaded. When sexism, racism or prejudicial systems come into play and my significant other is feeling some type of way about it, honesty prevails in our discussions regarding these struggles and helps us support one another. If one's ethics are strong, I know that they will always try their best to do the right thing. To me, those are core needs that I require from a person.

As women, we must be capable of digging deeply into the moral compass of our own being. What are our morals? What do we stand for? What are we willing to give it all up for? What are those core cues? Those are the stepping-stones in helping you form a list of needs from your mate. And once you have that list, you can grow from there.

Reflections
Step 7
Just One More Hit: Emotional Relapse

_____

_____

_____

_____

_____

_____

_____

_____

_____

_____

_____

_____

_____

_____

_____

_____

_____

_____

_____

_____

_____

_____

_____

_____

_____

RELATIONSHIP
DEPENDENCY & OVERDOSE

Are You an Ex-oholic: Addicted to Toxic Relationships?

*O*ften times, I encounter women who continue to dabble in the same types of relationships. They have a certain prototype that consists of what society says, their own ideals, and Disney fairytales all mixed together. Their friend will say, "I know this person is different. I know they have a different name. I even know that they have a different social security number, but it's the same person." These women are complaining about the same things they complained about in their last relationship. They're not making any progress. They haven't upgraded to a better situation. They haven't even upgraded themselves! They enjoy a honeymoon period and then experience the same issues all over again.

If you can relate, then you're an ex-oholic: a serial ex collector. The problem is that you don't realize that you are the common denominator in these relationships, and you end up going back to the same thing, over and over again.

How do you prevent this from happening?

Looking at your own insecurity as a way of making deeper changes within yourself is a great place to start when trying to avoid making the same mistakes. One of the reasons why women keep falling into the same type of relationship is because we give off a vibe that a potential mate can sense.

Here is an example. You have two women. The first is very assured and maintains a very positive frame of mind. She's wearing a slinky, black dress, is very self-confident and is comfortable in her environment. The other woman has on the same slinky black dress, but is struggling with self-doubt. She puts the dress on because she thinks it helps complete her by validating her attractiveness. The first woman, on the other hand, knew she was cute before she even put the dress on and wore the dress with much more confidence.

Potential mates can sense the insecurities in one woman just as easily as they can pick up on the strength projected by another. If that potential mate is a predator, there're going for the woman that has the weakest vibe. Why? It's less work, and all the potential mate has to do is sweep in and play the rescuer. They think, "I'm going to come in and pretend to save the day. If I'm able to save the day, rescue you, fix or put a quick fix on whatever emotional need that you're having, then you'll think I'm the bomb." Going a step further, the predator thinks about his or her prey, "now you're indebted to me without recognizing you're indebted to me." Because we all have animalistic tendencies within us, emotional predators will often sniff out insecurities and prey on them just as an animal would.

A woman that is very self-confident, on the other hand, will receive very few suitors because the suitors know that they must approach her correctly given the aura of security and completeness that she gives off. Their game must mirror the strong woman's confidence.

Ladies, in order to stop falling into those same kinds of addictive, toxic relationships and get out of the ex-oholic cycle, you have to start making deeper changes within. Start by figuring out what insecurities you have and address them. If you're unable to address them on your own, go seek professional help. Invest in yourself. I know that certain cultures are against it, but to see a counselor or a therapist is a valuable investment. Rather than spending money on Mac lipstick, Tory Burch shoes, or that Dolce and Gabana handbag that costs $300.00, why not invest your money in something that gives you the hope, healing, and happiness you deserve? A therapist can help you identify what your insecurities are and help you figure out effective coping strategies. Then, having made changes within, you'll be wearing the dress, rather than letting the dress wear you.

Why Do You Keep Going Back?

Is it easier for us to go back to old relationships because we feel like we know what we are dealing with? Do we go back because we are still fixated on the potential of the person, thinking we can "change" them? Do we go back out of weakness or fear that we will never find anyone else?

Well it's simple. We go back because of the ease of familiarity. It's easier for us to go back to old relationships because we already know the issues, the breakdowns, the pros, and the cons. We have it figured out because we've lived it. Because no one wants to start over, we stay in dead-end relationships, afraid of having to open up and reveal the same intimate secrets to a new mate. We don't want to go through the process of questioning whether we are sharing too much information again, because many times, we aren't sure about how much is "too much." It can be very intimidating. Instead, we take the easy route and go back to an old relationship.

We also go back because we think that we can change that person. One of the biggest misconceptions that people make in relationships is that they can change their mate. People don't change in relationships, they compromise. When you start changing yourself for the relationship, it signals the beginning of the end. You're no longer being authentic and true to who you are, and eventually, you start resenting your significant other because you can't be who you want to be in front of them. You get mad and end up breaking up. People compromise in relationships for the better of the relationship, or because they love and care about that person.

The fear of not finding someone else can also play a major part in why we ultimately go back. Social media, magazines, family members, girlfriends, guy friends, and other outlets often contribute to these misconceptions. "You know you're not going to find anybody without any kids. You know you're not going to find anybody with good credit. You know you're not going to find anybody that has a good job and doesn't have baggage." These different things that we are told affect our belief systems. Because of that lurking, internal fear that we have as women, we tend to keep going back to the same relationships.

"I can fix it," we say, convincing ourselves that we aren't going to find anyone else. How do we avoid falling into this trap of pessimistic self-talk? Well, if you just broke up with someone, it was for a reason. Why are you going back? Let that marinate for a few seconds. For whatever reason, you decided that it wasn't going to work. Your mate either did something, or you identified something in them that wasn't healthy for you. Even if they broke up with you, there was a reason for it. Remember: people don't change. They compromise for the relationships that are important to them.

I've been in relationships that didn't work out because I wasn't willing to compromise on certain things. I'm okay with making compromises to be in my marriage now because we agree on them together. We're on that same level. When you break up with someone, you did it for a reason. Recognize that your reasons are valid. Recognize that the particular relationship you were in wasn't a healthy one for you. Then, start breaking down that relationship.

Ask yourself what some of the things were in the relationship that you don't want to repeat in the next one. That will help you start pointing out some of those areas that you may need to work on while also helping you to establish your deal breakers. Again, recognize that you can't change a person.

You do not have control over whether a person decides to compromise or not. You can only control yourself. When we start to recognize that we don't have control over other people, we learn to be strong and independent if they no longer want to be with us.   Once you have done the work needed for your own positive growth, recognize that someone who chooses to break up with you is simply not ready for you. That person was not designed for you, so why would you want them? That's like trying to force a square peg into a round hole. You don't want to do that.

Stop fearing that you'll never find anyone else. You were able to find your ex as well as the one before them, weren't you? It's not that you're not going to find anyone else, it's just that you'll be picking from a smaller pool because you are now basing your relationship on your needs and not your wants.

Honestly, if you're looking to spend your life with someone, there should only be a few that get that opportunity. Think about that for a moment.   If I'm going to spend the rest of my life with someone that's going to fit me, be the cherry on top, and be the best accessory that I have 24/7, it would be kind of awkward if there were 50 million of them. It would mean that I'm not an original piece, and that they're not original, either. Instead, we would all simply be carbon copies because everything is based on our wants. If you focus on your needs and your moral compass, you won't have to worry about never finding someone else.

RELATIONSHIP DEPENDENCY & OVERDOSE

Co-Dependency/Addiction

Is this familiar?

Both you and your mate are suffering from emotional addiction and are self-destructing together. You both know that this is an unhealthy place for you to be in, but prefer to be messed up together than be separate and heal individually. In feeding off each other's insecurities and holding each other down, you never really allow growth and healing to happen.

Co-dependency occurs when you and your mate are suffering from the same addiction. One of the main rules in AA (Alcoholics Anonymous) is that members cannot date within the support group because of the risk of compiling issues together. If you and other members have identical problems, being together will cause each other's relapse. The result will be suffering and self-destructive behavior. Two addicts together only make a stronger addict because your cravings are now doubled. While you are partially healing, you are also partially destroying one another.

Now you're in an unhealthy space, in a co-dependent relationship. Both of you are messing up together. It's difficult for you to come out on the right side because your "person" is on the left side. The things that you try to do to recover are short-lived because the safe place that's supposed to be your mate is a part of your addiction.

You end up feeding off each other's insecurities while occupying lower levels of status and placement in your life. Your mate is going through a struggle because he or she doesn't have high expectations for you. They're not there to inspire you to grow, change, or develop. They don't want you to go back to school. They don't want you to shift careers. They're not growing, changing, or developing. If you were to grow, change, or develop, you would see things that they can't see. Your vision would be clearer. Your scope would be broader than theirs. Your mate won't be hoping for you to expand because they want you to remain in the same place. Sadly, you're doing the same thing to them.

How do we avoid being destructive together?

First, identify the characteristics of your co-dependency. Start looking at the things from your past relationships and reflect on the common markers of your break-up. What were some of the things that you felt weren't fulfilled within that relationship? What were some of the behaviors that took place that you continued to rationalize?

Remember: we're the queens of rationalization. "Well you know they had a hard day at work so that's why they snapped at me. I guess I could have been a little bit more understanding of the situation." We start picking at our own faults and rationalizing the defects of others so that it makes sense to us, and end up pacifying our needs with bullshit. Recognize instead of rationalizing and call it like it is. "You know what, that behavior was unacceptable. My own behavior was unacceptable as well."

Take a look in the mirror and ask yourself, "If I were on the outside looking in, what would I think about that woman if she did that? What would I say if she dressed and carried herself in that way? If my aunt, sister, or mom, were to see me, what would they think about my behaviors? What would someone that I admire think?"

Stop allowing yourself to make excuses, and really examine the rationalizations that you use for being with another person. Acknowledging the dependency issues and common themes that appear in your relationships is the first step in overcoming co-dependency. Now that you are aware of the issues, you can't continue to excuse them. The veils have fallen off your eyes and your rationalizing stops now! Now that you are aware, you can put in the work to create effective strategies going forward.

Reflections
Step 8
Relationship Dependency & Overdose

REHAB & **RECOVERY**

Identify a Healthy Relationship and Set Boundaries

*I*n Step 8, we discussed setting expectations and recognizing deal breakers. Let's expound on this. First of all, you must ensure that your expectations are realistic and not idealistic. To do this, you must separate yourself from the masses. This means disconnecting from social media, environmental expectations, and family to really look at yourself as a woman.

What are some things that you need? What do you require as a woman? Don't focus on what society or everyone else around you says that you require.

For example, as a single, thirty-two year old woman with a Ph.D., I was told by my family and society that I needed to be with someone that was of the same caliber as me. Expectations relating to the person I was supposed to be dating were very specific, stating, "That person needs to at least have a master's degree," "You don't have any kids, so they shouldn't have any kids," or, "They need to at least be making this much money." Society had outlined these guidelines for me, but when I started looking at the people that I had been with, I recognized that I had dated people across the board.

From blue-collar to white-collar, and six figures to two figures, I had dated them all. A few of the common requirements I had that I knew were non-negotiable, was that the person I dated had to be a hard worker, respect me, have morals, and be honest with me. When I began to recognize what my expectations were, they became the baseline for the people that I met and dated. If an individual happened to make six figures or had no kids that was just an added bonus.

I also set boundaries, and stuck with them. As women, sometimes we don't do this because we set boundaries, and then compromise on them. Though it's okay to compromise on things once your baseline or basic needs have been met, compromising your basic needs should never happen.

If I dated someone that had more than one child, I knew that it was a deal breaker for me. It was hard as hell-- especially if he was making six figures! I was like "Yo, we can work through the kids because we got these six figures." If I had continued with this kind of thinking, I wouldn't have been sticking to the moral compass of needs that I required for a healthy and complete relationship. I would have begun to backslide with the first compromise of my basic needs and would eventually have compromised over and over again.

I became honest with myself and said, "Okay if they don't fit these particular baseline criteria, they are not the person for me". I dated people that had more than one child, but it was not my cup of tea. Though all the other things in the relationship looked great, they didn't negate the baseline issues that I knew were deal-breakers. It would have been a waste of time going into the relationship thinking I could overlook these things, and wouldn't have been fair to me or the person I was dating.

When your boundaries have been set, you must recognize the red flags and follow through. Flags are red. They're not burgundy or pink, honey, they're red. Fire engine red! When you see a red flag that violates your standards as a person, it means it's time to put the brakes on that connection. We start seeing red flags in the beginning of relationships but often overlook them. However, when we sit back and look at our relationships afterword, we say, "Damn, that sure was a red flag." We know the red flags when we see them. We know them when someone is a little bit too extra, or when they're drinking a little bit too much, acting a fool. Honey, those are red flags that I don't tolerate. They are part of my baseline criteria. Therefore, if I'm dating someone and he begins to drink to the point where he can't control himself, I'm out. Deuces!

I'm gone because I know that is not something I can tolerate. That might be something that someone else is willing to work with, but not this girl, and not you either. Keeping track of those realistic expectations, recognizing those red flags, and then following through does not make you weak. It strengthens you as a woman, makes you more assertive, and puts you in a more powerful position where you are able to stick to your guns and say, "Yes, these are things that I require. These are needs that must be met in order for us to continue in this relationship."

Healing Past Childhood Trauma (Therapy)

The next thing that we must do is to heal past childhood trauma. This is a huge one. Childhood trauma is a major issue for women. We try to engage in new relationships, but we fail to heal from past trauma. Instead, we simply move past the trauma. Healing and moving are two different things. I can move to a different city. I can move to a different job. I can move to a different apartment, right? Out of sight, out of mind. However, I haven't healed. I haven't worked through that process. What we do to survive trauma is distract ourselves with projects. We distract ourselves with people, becoming nurturing rescuers and fixers for others. We immerse ourselves in our jobs, the corporate world, our churches, religion, yoga, and anything else that will occupy our time and attention.

We become addicted to those areas because we don't want to deal with our past trauma. Suddenly, your emotional tank gets full and spills over into everything. Like a domino effect, you end up bringing these negative emotions into all those areas that you built up.

Sometimes the trauma can be sexual or physical; other times it can be mental or emotional. Usually, women can recognize the first two forms of abuse. The mental and emotional abuse are tougher to recognize. They often take place in childhood and are the main reasons why we are emotional addicts now. We try to use our significant others to heal the emotional wounds that we got from our mothers and fathers, but are never really able to do so. Our solution is to substitute and connect with people that we think are going to help us feel good about ourselves.

Unfortunately, those are short term fixes. It's not fair for someone else to be responsible for healing your past trauma; it's up to you. That may mean going back to your mother or father and addressing the trauma with them face-to-face.

They may be deceased, so what do you do then? You still talk to them. You place the responsibility where it needs to be, saying to them--whether in spirit or in person-- "what you did was wrong, and it hurt me. I am no longer going to carry that responsibility for that hurt. I will transfer that hurt and pain back to you."

You put the responsibility on them, which means forgiving yourself, not forgiving them. Forgiveness is not about other people. Forgiveness is about you. You forgive the fact that you have allowed yourself to be controlled emotionally by another person. Despite the fact that person has passed away or moved on with their lives, you continue to carry emotional baggage from the trauma they inflicted upon you. You must forgive yourself for holding onto this pain. You release yourself from the trauma. Give yourself permission to heal, saying, "I'm going to live in the now". That is a choice that we can make for ourselves once we recognize the trauma. Oftentimes, getting past the pain requires seeking some type of therapy, which can be heavy and even involve major and minor setbacks. But like I said before, setbacks are just set ups for a come-back. It's necessary for us to sometimes break down the wall we built in order to reconstruct it with a stronger foundation.

Single, Not Alone

We discussed how being single doesn't mean being alone. There are differences in being alone and lonely. You have all these other areas in your life that you have now built up for yourself. You've added quality to your life. You recognize that you, not your mate, is what completes you. We watch movies where they say "You complete me." Chile', no they don't. The problems you had when you came into their life are the same problems you have leaving them. The happiness you had coming into the relationship should be the same happiness you have leaving it.

A mate is an extension of your life. They're not the absolute value of your life. Remember, my husband to me is one of my best accessories. He's a great asset. He's an extension to my greatness, and I am an extension of his. However, we can both live without each other. Individually we make the choice not to. What makes you great is knowing that you can live without a person, even though you would rather not. That's the difference.

Recognize that you have people in your circle who are supportive. That's what you need even if you are not in a relationship. This is the time to focus on yourself as an individual. You have time now to build your brand, to exercise, to complete some goals that you've had for yourself. Focus on becoming the best you. Once you start, that person that's out there waiting for you will show up immediately. When you stop focusing on everything else and start focusing on yourself--building your empire, growth, and legacy as a beautiful woman, your mate will show up and become the significant accessory that you need.

Reflections
Step 9
Rehab & Recovery

STEP 10

SEVEN AND **SEVEN**

Identifying a Healthy Relationship

*Y*ou are probably feeling super empowered now. The research has been done, and you've started the healing process. You may be at the point where you feel, "I might be ready for a relationship." But do you know how to be in a relationship? Although we've set our deal breakers, established our moral compass, and know what we're willing to compromise on, there is still more to do.

There are seven basic habits that we need in order to connect in our relationships as well as seven that we need to destroy. Understand that although we have done the work to start healing our emotional addiction, as human beings, we're still fallible creatures. Our emotions can be unstable; we have stressful and overwhelming moments, and our old behaviors may still resurface. For us to keep the process going and keep working on them, we have to look at 14 areas that we're able to clearly recognize as being positive or negative. These stem from seven deadly and seven connecting habits that we find in relationships.

7 Deadly Habits that Destroy Relationships	7 Connecting Habits
Criticizing	Caring
Blaming	Trusting
Complaining	Listening
Nagging	Supporting
Threatening	Negotiating
Punishing	Befriending
Manipulating	Encouraging

According to Dr. William Glasser, noted psychiatrist and author of numerous books, all relationships have the same fundamentals.

When we behave in a manner that yields deeper connections between two parties, we are engaging in connecting habits. On the other hand, if we act in a way that discourages connection in relationships, we are promoting one or more of the seven deadly habits.

Seven Deadly Habits

The first two deadly habits are **Criticizing** and **Blaming.** Are we constantly criticizing others? Are we criticizing ourselves? Sometimes we can be our own worst critic. Before anyone even tries to point things out to us, we're pointing them out. We may even be pointing out things that, by now, are insignificant. It's important that we take a moment to see what our criticizing and blaming behaviors are. Are we blaming people for things that they didn't do? Are we accepting blame for behaviors that are not our responsibility? When we get into these relationships, we often become so happy that we stop doing the work. Do we complain? I don't know how many times I've seen people get into relationships they wanted to be in only to start complaining all the time. "They're so aggravating! They just want to do this, and they want to do that." Wait a damn minute! Isn't that what you asked for? Didn't you ask for someone to be there for you, spend time with you, and want to do things with you? Suddenly, now that you have what you asked for, you're not satisfied.

Nagging. There is nothing wrong with pointing out a concern, or having a discussion about a situation or issue, but nagging can sometimes discourage a person from wanting to engage at all. If I ask my husband, "Honey, when are you going to clean the pool?" And he says, "I'll clean it this weekend," for him, that may mean Friday, Saturday, or Sunday. Friday comes.

"You going to clean the pool?"

"I'm going to clean it this weekend."

Saturday comes.

"When are you going to clean the pool?"

Now, he's mad, and he doesn't want to clean the pool because I nagged him. Remember not to be overly pushy in your relationship and allow your mate the opportunity to show you what they can do.

Mothering (this one I added, because we totally do this ladies). There would be more positive energy in your relationships if you didn't feel like you needed to mother the relationships. Because women are nurturers, they tend to play the mother in their relationships. We tend to stand over our mates like children, making sure and demanding they do things just right or that they follow through. What we aren't realizing is that more can get done when we request rather than demand that our mates complete a task. When you request and give them the opportunity to do something and show appreciation for their efforts, you strengthen their willingness to participate. The next time, you won't even have to request it.

Threatening. "If you don't do this, I'm going to do this!" Such conflicts may involve dangling the words "divorce" or "I'll leave you" whenever you're in an argument. These are unnecessary tactics that get old quickly. No one responds well to a threat. Initially the person may comply with what you are asking because of the threat, but it is done out of animosity and tension instead of love. If you continue to resort to threats, your mate is going to give you what you think you want, responding with, "Divorce me! Leave me! Let me help you pack!". Because that response isn't what you truly want, you are now in distress. You were just using the threats to control the situation.

Punishing. Some women may become upset with my thoughts on this subject, but that doesn't matter. You can't stop being the type of woman that you have established yourself as just because your mate stops being who they once were. Doing so would be back-stepping: reverting back to a previous form of yourself that you have worked very hard to overcome.

For example, my husband and I have had rough patches. You're going to have rough patches in your relationships. One of the things that I remember not doing, which I had done in previous relationships (I can't talk about it if I haven't lived it) is choosing to stop washing dishes, or stop washing my mate's clothes when he did something wrong. I would resort to really petty behavior, such as cooking a meal for one. Meanwhile, I think I'm punishing him, right? I think I'm making it hard for him, and initially I am. The person gets mad and you feel good. They don't have any clean underwear, and you think you are unleashing a proper punishment. However, what you're really doing is showcasing an individual that's not you. You're being that woman that you have worked so hard to never be again. You're becoming someone that you despise and killing your character.

I don't believe in punishing people in relationships. If the relationship is not working out, you don't punish the other person, you get out of the relationship. I'm not going to turn into an evil bitch trying to punish you. The best thing that I can do to show you that I'm strong is to leave you. That means that I'm stepping up and making good choices for myself. I'm not going to stop washing dishes or spend more time trying to separate your clothes from mine. I don't have time to do all that. I'm still going to be the remarkable woman that I am. If anything, I'm going to start cooking better meals to show you, "Honey, you really don't want to lose this." I'm going to do what my moral compass and standards tell me to do. Why? Because, at the end of the day, if my mate chooses to leave the relationship, or if I choose to leave, I can leave with a clear conscience. No regrets.

I didn't act a fool. I didn't pour oil in your shoes. I didn't set anything on fire. All of that is unnecessary. Those are character killers, and I'm certainly not about to go to jail for you. I'm not going to ruin everything that I built up because you don't want to get right. I'm going to keep building myself. As I stated before, as you build yourself, people will fall off. One of those people may be the person that you're in a relationship with.

Manipulating. Rewarding your mate in order to control the relationship is an easy way to think about manipulating. Now, we're talking about the P-U-S-S-Y, because that's a bargaining chip that I know is used frequently. Women use sex as a weapon of manipulation to control their mate by performing sexual acts or getting their partner hot and bothered just to gain compliance. The flip-side of this behavior is that women are degrading themselves sexually in return for a favor (i.e. having bills paid, hair and nails done, shopping trips, etc.).

Just because you're not on a street corner, doesn't mean that you are now not a prostitute. Instead, you've just become an in-house hooker. Unfortunately, many women will live that lifestyle. "Let me go over here and break such and such off because you know I need my hair done or my light bill paid." We even disregard their marital status. Women will purposely do certain sexual favors with another woman's husband or wife to get something out of it. That's a problem. Eventually that wears out and is no longer enough to keep your mate interested, involved, or financially invested.

What will you do then?

You do not have to subject yourself to sexual games or any other degrading behavior. You shouldn't have to bribe or manipulate unconditional love. Examples from previous chapters illustrate many of the seven deadly habits we've discussed here.

Seven Connecting Habits

Caring. Caring is the first connecting habit. You have to give a shit about your partner and about yourself. You must care enough about yourself to not allow your mate to disrespect and walk all over you. You also must care enough about them to tell them if they are doing something that you think is disrespectful. This often involves engaging in difficult conversations, but in demonstrating care by speaking up, you can turn care into trust, the next connecting habit.

Trust. It's important to not only trust your partner, but also trust yourself with your partner. If you don't have trust in a relationship, you might as well end it. Trusting someone involves giving them the opportunity and responsibility to hold you up and keep you safe. That's a huge responsibility, and one that you must take on as well. You can't build trust if you're still holding on to anger and hate from previous relationships. Instead, you have to trust that your partner will do the right thing and that when they make big decisions, they're going to make those decisions with you in mind.

Listening. Listening is another important connecting habit. It's critical that you listen to what your significant other has to say and hear them out completely before responding. Sometimes, we're so focused on formulating a rebuttal that our brain is missing half of what our partner is saying to us. As a therapist, part of my job involves providing feedback, but the most important responsibility that I have is to listen. If I don't listen, I won't be able to pick out certain things that my clients say subconsciously that could help them grow or overcome an obstacle. Listening may also mean that you must repeat what the person says to make sure you heard it correctly. Sometimes, what our mate says to us and what we hear them say are two different things.

Sometimes we hear things differently because our minds are preoccupied, or we're not focused. We hear things differently because what is being said sounds similar to something we've already heard in the past. Our brains have these automatic receptors that start filtering and coming up with answers and solutions, which can sometimes get in the way of active listening. When having a conversation with your mate about what they need, listen to them and repeat what they say.

For instance, one of the things that my husband has said in the past was that I undermine him. At first, when I wasn't listening, I responded, "I'm not undermining you. What are you talking about? I don't undermine you. Are you kidding me? I support you. I'm here for you. I cook. I clean. What do you mean?" He responded, "There are things that I tell you that I'm going to take care of, and if I don't take of care of it in your timeframe, you do it yourself. And that undermines me as a man." I had to sit and listen. Several things he said stood out to me.

The first was him saying, "Your timeframe," meaning that I was basing his actions off my own timeframe. On the surface, that assumption is ridiculous. It would be ass backwards to base my expectations for what he does on my timeframe. And when I did go ahead and do the things that I had requested he do, his interpretation became, "What the hell does she need me for?"

I had to listen to what he was telling me at that time. I had to apologize. Not just apologizing to say, "I'm sorry," But also vowing not to do that shit again. You can't listen, apologize, and then repeat the same ignorant behavior. Apologies are only worth anything if appropriate actions follow. Listening is very important. Sometimes it's good to listen when your mate is not even aware that you're listening. An example of this could be when they're not talking to you. Maybe they're talking to a co-worker or a friend, but you overhear certain things that they're struggling with. Listen to those things your spouse says-- to you or to someone else--and then try to support them in those areas.

Supporting. Supporting doesn't mean doing everything for them. It means being there if they fall and helping them to get back up. That's support. Supporting is your mate coming home and saying, "I got laid off today," and you say, "Do you need help updating your resume? What do we need to do? What are you interested in? What are your next steps going to be? Let's figure this out together." That's supporting. Support isn't them coming home and saying, "I got laid off" and you replying with "Why did you get laid off? What did you do? You know we got bills." Don't you think they know that? They were almost afraid to come home and tell you they got laid off. You can't kick them when they're down, you have to support them, letting them know that you're going to stand by them and be there to help them work through the hardships. Sometimes, support doesn't always come in a physical form. Support can be spiritual through prayer, meditation or the sending out good vibes.

Support can be you. My husband works the overnight shift, and when he comes home it's usually four in the morning. Sometimes he doesn't get to bed until six, after he has taken time to wind down. At the same time, because we have a two-year-old, I usually get up at seven. When this happens, I try to show support by turning the baby monitor off, waking our child up, and we going to a room in the back of the home away from where my husband is sleeping. I'll try to run errands during the day and do whatever is necessary to keep the house quiet, so that he can rest and be able to function at work later on. Such considerations are what being supportive looks like in action. Paying attention to your mate's struggles and doing small things to show support indicates that you care and can make a difference.

Negotiating. I also call this debating. Negotiating is important. When you're in a relationship, there's no room for "I decided," or "I made the choice." Being in a relationship means that you have to relate to one another in order for the ship to sail smoothly. Negotiating involves both of you bringing something to the table and equally weighing the pros and cons of it. You may not always agree, but through the negotiating process, you can come up with an acceptable middle-ground. You can collectively decide on acceptable ideas that work for both of you. Let me go back to the topic of my husband working nights.

Because he works six days a week, one of the negotiations that I made, was as follows: "Honey, I know you need your rest, however, I would like to spend some quality time with you before you go to work" (before I brought this up, he tended to sleep in until it was time to go to work again). My request was that for 3 days out of the week when he's working the night shift, he would wake up a little bit earlier so that we could have a few hours together before he went off to work.

With a bit of negotiating, we were able to compromise. I agreed that if he worked on the weekend, he could wake me up when he came in from work and we go watch the sunrise outside together, or we take a bath together. The baby would still be sleeping, and we could share quality time together. Those were all negotiations that we made to be sure that we got our quality time together as a couple. Because our work shifts were opposite, the adjustments were a necessary compromise to help support our marriage. In the end, negotiation and sacrifice are necessary from both parties in order to get the most out of your relationship.

Befriending. I honestly believe befriending should be number one. Being your mate's friend is important because the friendship is something that grows as the relationship grows. You don't become BFFs (Best Friends Forever) immediately out the gate; it takes some time for your relationship to reach those heights. As your relationship grows, though, your mate should also be growing as your best friend. A lot of people confuse what a best friend is. "Oh, my mate is my best friend, my boo." Some married couples, and even those that aren't married, often suggest that their mates or significant others are their best friends. This connection is not always true among couples, as being a mate is not the same thing as being a best friend. There are things that you may tell your best friend that you don't tell your mate. I'm not saying that everyone shouldn't have an outlet. Everyone has that girlfriend or guy friend that knows your deep, dark, and ugly secrets. We need those friends. We're able to stay in our relationships because our friends know the deep, dark, and ugly, and we're able to vent to them about the ins and outs.

However, what I mean by befriending is that if something great happens to you, the first person you should want to call is your mate, because they're your best friend. I knew my husband was my best friend when I responded in this manner. It may seem minor, but the minor things can quickly become majorly important.

I'm a bit of a shoe whore, and I remember an experience when my husband and I were in the mall one day. I saw this pair of Michael Kors boots that I wanted, but they were clearly out of my price range. I've got caviar taste on a tuna budget. I remember he and I were looking at them and I was like, "Maybe next time." About 2 weeks later, I went to the mall, saw a 75% sale, and had a coupon for the store. You couldn't tell me I wasn't doing it. I was able to get those boots for like $75.00.

The first thing I did was call my husband:

"Baby, guess what?"

"What?"

"I got those shoes for like $75.00. Can you believe it?"

You know that's a BFF conversation, right? That's a conversation that you have with your best friend. However, my husband is my best friend, and I called him first. It may have been about something simple like a pair of shoes, but to me, that experience was significant because it highlighted important components of my best friend relationship. Now, because I was able to nurture the friendship with my husband, I call him on a regular basis to consult with him on a variety of topics and decisions.

Encourage. We talked about being supportive, but it's equally important to encourage your mate. Encouraging each other establishes the positive reinforcement previously noted, that I noted can be lacking sometimes in our relationships. Encouragement lets your mate know they did an awesome job. I don't care how old you are, you like to be recognized for your good work, whether it's on your job, or by your parents. It doesn't matter what it is. We, as human beings, like positive reinforcement. We like positive energy. The problem is that we don't do it a lot. We don't give it out. We don't reciprocate it. When you encourage your mate, it makes them feel valued in the relationship. It also motivates them to reciprocate the very same encouragement by motivating them to go even harder at the things that they were doing before.

When my husband does a chore like cleaning the floors, I'll say, "Honey, the floors look awesome. You did a really good job. They look great!" He may act like it doesn't matter, but guess who'll be singing and humming while they clean the floors next time? Just that little bit of encouragement is everything. If I'm trying to eat healthier and my husband and I go to a restaurant and he says, "Well honey, they've got some good salmon and vegetables on this menu--you could order that," his words serve as encouragement for me and he becomes a part of my plan.

It's about providing encouragement and positive reinforcement to one another, giving praise and expressing your appreciation, and calling at random to say: "I appreciate you for who you are, for what you do, and for what you bring to this relationship. Thank you for being a good spouse." Express thanks to your partner for being a good mom, or a good mate. Leave notes on their car or pack their lunch.

The little things matter. You know, I'm a professor. So on the first day of classes, my husband will make me a little breakfast and put a note alongside it saying things like "To the best teacher ever, have a good day, honey. I love you." He does this sporadically, and it means the world to me. I still have all those damn notes. They are the little pieces that I think about when I sometimes want to run him over with a lawnmower. When you're pissed off with your mate, remembering past sweet gestures and expressions help to balance the relationship.

In relationships, if we can conquer the little things and handle those with as much positivity and love as possible, we're better prepared to handle the big things when they come along. As a result we're unified, and we encourage each other as we present our best selves in the relationship.

Reflections
Step 10
Seven and Seven

STEP 11

ABSTINENCE:
Maintaining Emotional Sobriety

$\mathcal{S}$o, you've identified the positive and negative aspects of relationships. You have your moral compass. You're working through your healing, your trauma, and your past. Society's views don't guide you. You've become very introspective and focused on self-care. How do you maintain all this growth? This step is here to help guide you further.

As I stated, some friendships will fall off on their own. In other cases, you'll have to let go of unhealthy friendships. Some of the people around you are so busy doing wrong that they don't want to see you doing right. They recognize that you're growing and they're not. Eventually, they will no longer feel that they have a place in your world and they'll exit, stage left. However, other individuals will hang around just to see what's going on. Sometimes, we must let go of those friendships and even family members, in extreme cases. If there's a toxic person that's been in your life forever (whether they're family or friends), it doesn't mean that they should be there for the second chapter of your growth. Letting go of the toxic people and things in your life will allow you to continue to invest in yourself while surrounding yourself with positive people and things. Family can be especially hard to let go of because the concept of blood relations creates a sentimental block. As they say, "Blood is thicker than water." You might say, "She may have treated me like shit, but that's still my mom." Though it doesn't mean that you have to stop speaking to them entirely, it's important to recognize which members of your family are toxic and shouldn't play an integral role in your life moving forward.

Every person in your life should occupy a unique place. You are the core. You are the center of this circle. Surrounding you are the people that you are closest to. As you extend out another layer, there's the next group, followed by another after that. You may find that you need to push certain people back a few layers, meaning that you may not talk to your mom everyday if she's always a "Negative Nancy." Likewise, you may not need to talk to your friend everyday if he or she constantly comes with baggage attached. You may want to stop calling that friend who always seems to have something wrong every time you speak to them.

You may need to save those interactions for once every week or so. Pay attention to those family members or friends that are always complaining, sad, or just plain nosy. Those are red flags.

Sometimes we have to let go of those friendships and unhealthy family relationships in order to maintain positivity. If not, those negative relationships will eventually wear you down. You will begin to become engrossed in their issues and will start saying, "yes" to them and "no" to yourself.

Next, you must get rid of the items that are reminders

of the old you. Why do you have a box of old photos or old pictures in your phone? If you've moved past the relationship, you should be able to get rid of all those sentimental items that were connecting you to a previous partner. That person is now a part of your past, and if that relationship is over, you must move forward and turn the page on that chapter.

Now, I have scrap books that contains pictures of me and ex-boyfriends. You know where they are located? Those scrapbooks are in the bottom of my closet. They don't necessarily mean anything. They're just a part of my past, and that's fine. If you have things that you're holding on to, little tokens, mementos that you look at that take you back to a certain time, I need you to throw that shit away. These things only bring you down and cause you to reminisce about what could have, should have, or would have been. They are triggers that pull us back to negative emotional and addictive states.

Just as you mature, so should your look. We all know women who claim to have matured but still wear clothes that scream immature and desperate. Bless their hearts. For the rest of us, what you wear and how you present yourself to the world changes with growth. Your environment and those mementos should change as well. Honey, you have to start letting go and getting rid of all those connections that pull you back. You must start presenting yourself as the powerful and assertive woman you are. Now don't get me wrong, there's a time and a place for that slinky dress and cut off shorts. However, that shouldn't be the primary way your light shines in the world.

While we're on the subject, why do you still have their phone number in your phone, huh? You don't plan on calling them again, so there's no need to keep their number. If you are keeping a number, it's normally your go-to person, the one we kind of bounce back to in between relationships. Once you decide to break the cycle of emotional addiction, you no longer need to go back to your old emotional drug or person of choice. You can put that down. There isn't a need to revisit that time because your emotional highs now come from you rather than from another person.

Also, recognize that this is all one, long process and celebrate each of the small steps that you're taking. Let's say you go through some of your photos and you can only bring yourself to getting rid of four or five of them. Celebrate that! A few months ago, you couldn't get rid of a damn thing. Now you have just let go of four or five! Maybe it's the stuffed animal that they won for you at the carnival. Let it go! Donate it to charity, or recycle it by giving it to another person. Those mementos are great, but now they hold a different meaning. You should celebrate those small successes. Celebrate those opportunities that show you've grown. Recognize that you're achieving your goals, even if it's just a small step.

I once was in a very long-term relationship. We were engaged, and it didn't work out. I was crushed and blindsided by it not working out. After I went through a full year of cleansing, detoxing and working on myself, I started revisiting the places that reminded me of him, but also began associating new memories with those places.

One of our spots was Cold Stone Creamery, an ice cream store. I would say, "I can't go to Cold Stone because that was our spot." Well, I got some of my best girlfriends and a group of us went to Cold Stone and ate. Now my newest and best memory of Cold Stone is my girlfriends and I cracking up with laughter while mixing all those different flavors. I chose to make my memories of that place be something that I wanted to remember and had a great time doing so. It's not that I forgot that he and I went there, but now he and I going to Cold Stone isn't as prominent as the awesome time that I had with my girlfriends.

You can replace initial emotions with new emotions. I've done that with many things. I've traveled to places repeatedly and experienced new memories. I've been able to embrace new places and cultures because I detached older, negative memories from them. That has been a step that I have taken throughout my life to help me overcome difficult memories.

This approach also works with memories caused by music. At one point, I dated a guy and Anthony Hamilton was all we would listen to; and you know Anthony Hamilton gets you in your feelings. For a while, every time one of his songs came on, I couldn't listen. Eventually, I started listening to Anthony Hamilton in different environments where I was enjoying myself. I bobbed to the music and allowed myself to attach positive emotions to the music rather than allowing the negative "woe is me" feelings to linger because I heard our song. By doing little tricks like these, I set myself free from allowing my emotions to control the music that I listened to, and have enjoyed the same success in overcoming negative emotions that were tied to places, situations, and people.

Let's talk about counseling because this is important. Counseling is not just for someone who is having a mental breakdown. Counseling is not just for someone that we deem "crazy" or unstable. Counseling and therapy exist for you to get non-biased insight into your thinking process. Sometimes counseling is there to provide you confirmation that assures you that you're making the right decision. Whatever you use counseling for, you just want to make sure you get a clear, non-biased perspective.

We must get past the misconception that counseling or therapy is only for people that have mental issues. Eighty percent of my clients have no diagnosis. They come to me because they're struggling with relationship or growth issues and ask, "Where am I right now in my life, and where should I be going from here?" People want to know how to heal from a past relationship, or get along with someone unpleasant at their job. Those are problems that counseling, and therapy can help with. Sometimes we need someone with a clear perspective to open our eyes and help us to recognize the destructive behavioral paths we're traveling down.

Those things really help with the long-term abstinence of emotional addiction and making amends. Therapy can take place in many ways. Face-to-face therapy is a plus, and I am always available to help further in that regard. There is also virtual therapy, which includes Skype, email, and over-the-phone counseling. When you are traveling down this road toward your "best you," there are options. You can do it from the comfort of your home or car. The process of healing takes time. You may have spent 15-20 years in a negative space, so it is going to take some time to get out of that space. And that is perfectly okay. Every month that you have growth is a month where you are winning. Don't rush the healing process. Remember: it is your healing, not anyone else's.

Reflections
Step 11
Abstinence: Maintaining Emotional Sobriety

_____

_____

_____

_____

_____

_____

_____

_____

_____

_____

_____

_____

_____

_____

_____

_____

_____

_____

_____

_____

_____

_____

_____

STEP 12

SELF-CHECKS

*I*n my life and therapy practice, I try to approach things with a realistic perspective. The goal is to address all areas of healing to find complete inner-happiness, while remembering to always include self-checks. Self-checks are simple strategies that you can use to stay in tune with your emotional sobriety. These checks help you to maintain accountability and not fall too far off track. Here are a few suggestions to get you started and help you maintain emotional sobriety.

1. Purchase a journal. I was once asked in an interview, "If you could recommend a book to your clients, what would it be?" I replied, "A blank journal." Naturally, people were totally confused. "Who's the author of that?" I was asked. "You are!"

The reason why I'm so adamant about journaling is that no one can tell your story like you can. Nothing hits you harder than your own words. I keep journals, and write in them every week. It's interesting to go back and not only look at the progress that I have made, but also find patterns in my behavior. At times, I've come across things that I said I would fix six months ago that I'm still doing today. Journals are not only great for positive reinforcement, but they're also a great way of checking to see if you're still struggling with negative habits from the past.

It's a great way for us to go back and improve in some areas. Once you learn the formula of success for your life, that formula is the same for everything. You must apply it. Writing in your journal makes you aware of how you're feeling about something because it's the one space in which we are pretty much always honest. We can expose ourselves in our journals because we know that the content is private and that no one else will read it. We're allowed to be vulnerable.

I'll even have clients write in their journals as an assignment and then bring it in so we can review some of it. Initially, clients may have difficulty disclosing their issues verbally due to this being a new therapeutic relationship. When I can step into their journals, it gives me insight into their thought processes when they're alone. I'm able to learn what they think about, and can help them recognize patterns when they start to rationalize things by distorting their own thinking. Journals are an informative way of keeping a log of our progress and successes.

2. Recognize Patterns. I have my clients come up with a list. They list the names and characteristics of their most serious relationships and jot down the positives and negatives of each relationship on a separate sheet of paper. I'll do this over a period because I don't want the authentic emotion to be compromised. Each session will be about a different person. In a few months, we'll come together with all the lists and start to compare them. That helps my clients to recognize the prototype that they've presented. This is a great eye-opener for people as well because they've had separate opportunities to list the good and bad characteristics of each individual. What we find is that their bad characteristics are similar.

We also begin to consider the mate selection process. It gives us an idea of our assertiveness in the relationship. Did you find a pattern? Who did all the initiating in the relationships? Did they like the same types of hobbies? Was this a relationship where you felt desperate all the time? Did you feel bored? Were you anxious? These are all emotional factors that you describe.

After examining the characteristics of these relationships and of the people in them, you notice these patterns about yourself. Once you start picking up on these patterns, you're like, "Okay that was a "me" issue, not a "them" issue. "I need to start working on how I cannot come across as desperate. Why do I get anxious when I have to inquire or ask questions? "Why do I feel like I'm in competition all the time with other women?" If you're finding examples like these to be common in every single relationship, it means they are personal, internal attributes, not external ones.

3. Write memos to yourself. I love sticky notes. Positive sticky notes are awesome because you can put them anywhere. When I've gone through my own struggle, I put sticky notes in places to remind myself how awesome and great I was, or to remind myself that I'm going to make it through the day. I put them in places that I may look at all the time, but will also put some in places that I don't always look. I don't need as many sticky notes because I've gone through my process of healing, but I still use them as encouraging messages or as part of my mantra.

Sometimes I tuck notes in random shoes. That way, when I go to put a shoe on, there's a message in there that says, "Make today great; Today will be positive; or, You rock!" I make sure these notes are encouraging. When I find a note, it is always just what I needed. Even when I wasn't sad and found a note, the message gave me extra reassurance. On each of the notes, I made sure to write down the words that applied to my needs and insecurities.

You can write a memo to document how far you have come on your journey. We live in a technology age and use our phones for everything. I set up my phone at one time to send a reminder that I had been eating healthy for 2 weeks. I completely forgot that I had set it. When it came up, it was just the reinforcement I needed to keep me going.

4. Make connections. It's good to get to know people and genuinely try to have a positive impact on the lives of others daily. It changes how you feel about yourself, and it also has a positive impact on others. I try to do one positive task per week for someone else--often anonymously--just to let a person know that someone cares about them. This kind of "pay it forward" mentality is important.

Fostering supportive networks is another area of importance. I make sure that I keep a strong connection with some of my closest girlfriends, putting them on my calendar as a reminder to keep in touch. I remember a random person commenting on my putting my girlfriends on my calendar. They said, "Oh, you're so busy you got to schedule us in?". I replied, "The fact that you see it that way is kind of closed-minded because anything that's important in my life goes on my calendar. My doctor's appointments, business meetings, kid's appointments, anniversaries, and birthdays all go on that calendar."

When you think about it, all important reminders go on our calendars. Now, my group of friends have adopted a similar practice. We put each other on our calendars and schedule weekends with girlfriends. They become a part of my schedule.

It's easy for us to get overbooked and overwhelmed. We often take on other tasks that cause us to stop nurturing ourselves in our relationships. It's easy for us to fall into that trap. I try to make sure to foster those networks and support systems with old friends while also making new connections when I can.

If I'm at work and there's someone new, I'll say, "Hey we're going to lunch on Friday. You want to grab a bite with us?" You never know who may be a positive outlet in your life. Try to foster as many environments full of life as you can, because those environments just build added positivity for you.

5. Complete your sentences.

I see myself as...

The most important thing about me is...

I can...

I feel...

What I dislike most about a person is...

I try to be...

I get angry if...

I feel the most joy when...

I believe in...

I want to accomplish...

What I like most about myself is...

I dislike it when...

I should...

I don't feel like myself when...

I am weakest when...

These queries kind of go along with your mantra that I talked about in the previous steps. This is where we're taking the things that are negative about ourselves and flipping them into something positive. If you read your responses every day, you're reading positivity into your life. Such self-checks are ways for us to make sure that we are on track and in tune with our needs. Though your basic moral compass may stay the same, your needs will change as you grow. When I was emotionally immature, I was more focused on a mate that could provide because at the time, I needed someone that made more than minimum wage. I wanted to live comfortably and be able to afford the basics. Now that I've grown, I don't necessarily need that. I want financial security, but I don't need anyone else to provide that for me.

One thing that's very clear is that as you complete this process of emotional growth and investment in yourself, your perception of your needs will change. You may even realize that they were really just "wants." These little sentences help you stay in tune with your goals and the progress you've made toward them.

I love the one that says, "I believe in." What do you believe in? You don't have to necessarily make it a spiritual question, but can keep it general instead. I believe that people are generally good. Those are all things that we can keep reflecting on that help us to revise our plans of attack as we continue to grow. We've got to revisit, check, and re-answer these questions constantly. As we grow, things change. One of the sentences says, "I get angry when . . ." If you're in the process of getting through your healing, you might say, "I get angry when my mate doesn't follow through in a timely manner. Now that you've gone through your process, you've figured out that you were basing everything on your own timeframe. You'll notice that the things that cause you to get angry change because growth has taken place.

6. Be aware of your body. It's important that we pay attention to our body's signals of when we are not emotionally healthy. In the beginning of this book, I touched on how our negativity and toxins affect our body, muscles, digestive systems, accuracy, and energy level. I also talked about how our vibes and auras sometimes

Dr. Carleah East

121

attract people to us that we should avoid. Being aware of our bodies and how they are aligned is essential to how we operate. You're not effective if you are not feeling your best. Exercise and healthy eating is important.

I'm not going to sit up here and front. I love a cheeseburger and some fries. I like me a slab of ribs. I'm an emotional eater like the next person. For me to function to the best of my abilities, I can't eat those things every day. I like a glass of wine and some Hennessy on ice, but I can't drink that every day either. There are things that we must do in moderation. When I go hard all week, I like to reward myself. When I do my best to eat healthy and to do some type of physical activity, whether it's washing my car, or vacuuming the house, or going to the gym, or just taking a walk, on the weekend, I allow myself a drink or two. I allow myself those meals because I worked hard during the week. When I know that my body is getting out of whack, my breathing is different, and my heart is beating faster than it should be, those are signs that I'm getting anxious or panicky, and need to calm down. I do a self-assessment that very moment. Why is my heart beating so fast? Why am I anxious about this? Is it something that I can control? That's the key. We must recognize that our emotions often manifest in our bodies, and our bodies respond in certain ways. It is okay to hit the pause button and allow yourself the opportunity to check those areas.

7. Thought Stopping. When your brain is on a cycle of a thought process and you begin to get upset, you experience thought stopping. You're getting ready to be annoyed. You feel yourself becoming anxious, panicky, and getting scared. Suddenly, you "thought stop." You push the timeout button and you say, "Wait. I'm recognizing that I'm upset. I'm recognizing that I'm pissed. What am I really pissed about right now? Am I mad about what just took place, or is there something else that I'm mad about that's adding to this aggression? Is this something I should be mad about? How does this affect me? How can I overcome this?" Thought stopping techniques, such as these, can be very useful in helping us to control our emotions when we become upset.

I recommend this strategy to clients because it allows us to trigger an emotion but stop ourselves before we start cycling through all of the other nonsense that can affect our moods and well-being. When we generate that trigger, we recognize it as a trigger, and are able to start using effective coping strategies to tackle it head-on. Different forms of thought stopping might range from exercise and practicing forgiveness to recognizing that we simply don't have control over the situation we're in. That's what separates us. That's what defines us as survivors. In the beginning, we see ourselves as victims, but through growth, we become survivors. In the end, our mission is to become thrivers.

A victim is a person that is still struggling with addiction and abuse. A survivor is a person that has lived past the abuse and the emotional addiction, but may not have fully taken control of their lives. A thriver is someone who has undergone marked growth and transformation and is now the master of the elements of addiction and abuse that once controlled their lives.

Thrivers are able to learn new techniques and embrace

themselves as they are. They say "yes" to themselves and have become comfortable shedding old friendships, letting go of toxic relationships, and hanging up the phone on negative family members. Because of this, they are thriving and have successfully reached new heights, using thought stopping as a way to get in tune with their emotions.

8. Connect with a therapist. Various indicators can be useful in helping an individual determine if therapy is right for their specific case. For some, anxiety and panic attacks are a clear-cut signal. For others, a combination of factors including alcohol or substance addiction, problems at work, or difficulty maintaining a relationship can all be telling signs that professional help may be needed. In highly overt circumstances, some people are even told by friends and family that they need to see a therapist. Though these are all common factors that contribute to a client's choice to seek therapy, they may not apply to everybody. Not everyone has a trauma or struggles with substance abuse. Some clients may suffer from issues that aren't clearly laid out. They may say, "I just want to learn how to embrace myself. I want to learn how to love myself a little bit more. I'm married and I love my mate, but I want to spice up my marriage. I want to make my marriage better. I want to be the best wife that I can be to my mate." Some people just want to figure out what the hell they're doing with their lives.

There are a lot of people that go from one job to the next, but don't really know where they're going. I'm able to help clients figure out what their passions are and use that insight to help them connect to professions in which they can earn a living. The goal is for them to be happy with their lives and feel fulfilled professionally.

People go to therapists because they're trying to achieve new goals in a number of areas in their lives. Some people come to learn how to let go and forgive, while others look to become stronger, more assertive, and more expressive. For those that are mentally exhausted, therapy serves as an outlet through which to renew your mind, prepare yourself, receive much-needed positive reinforcement, and generally gain a new outlook on life.

Therapy incorporates a number of different human health areas apart from mere mental wellbeing. Each of these areas help us to maintain emotional sobriety for the rest of our lives by allowing us to come back to and readdress them as many times as we want. Will there be setbacks? Certainly. There will always be challenges in our lives that we have to overcome.

But guess what? You now have the tools to work through these issues. Everything that you learned can now be used as part of your arsenal in the fight to win your emotional sobriety. That is what's important about this whole process.

You now have a great place to start your emotional recovery. No more excuses. No more procrastination. No more distractions. It is time to start doing the work. No more Hangovers!

Reflections
Step 12
Self-Checks

ABOUT THE **AUTHOR**

*D*r. Carleah East, LMHC, native of St. Petersburg, Florida, is a Clinical Psychotherapist, Licensed Mental Health Counselor and Psychology Professor. She attended the University of Central Florida in Orlando for her Bachelor of Arts in Psychology with a minor in Sociology. She obtained a Masters of Arts in Mental Health Counseling from Argosy University and obtained her Ph.D. in General Psychology from Capella University.

Dr. East, aka "The Sapphire Woman", currently operates her private practice called S.M.I.L.E –Solving & Managing Issues w/ Love & Enrichment and is a Psychology Professor at St. Petersburg College. Along with healing minds and educating them, Dr. East promotes the strength of women in her many empowerment seminars and workshops. In her spare time, she enjoys volunteering, shopping and spending time with family and friends. Dr. East is someone who will go above and beyond to support her community. With laughter and love she encourages others to find happiness one day at a time.